Sins Destruction

Johnna B.

Watch My Journey Publications presents:
Sins of Destruction

This novel is a work of fiction. Any resemblances to real
people, living or dead, actual events, establishments,
organizations, or locales are intended to give the fiction a
sense of reality. Other names, characters, places, and incidents
are either products of the author's imagination or are used
fictitiously.

For information contact: watchmyjourneyjb@gmail.com

Author's email: Johnnab82@gmail.com
Cover Design by Karoz Norman
Editing: Joy Hammond-Nelson
Layout: Raynesha Pittman

ISBN: 978-0-692-63254-3
LCCN: LC001413299

DEDICATION

In loving memory of my angel, my love, my mother. I miss you with every piece of me. I never knew life could get so unbearable. I am lost in this big world without you. This book almost did not make its release because I knew how excited you were to read it. Now that you are gone I don't know how to feel right now. Nevertheless, I am going on and trying to stay strong the way you raised me to be. I love you and miss you so much my love. I pray I am making you proud, loving you always your Stephanie King.

Joycelyn thank yo again I hope you enjoy :)

John B

CONTENTS

THANK YOUS

I want to thank everyone for keeping me in your prayers when I had given up on everything. I appreciate you all from the bottom of my heart. Writing this book took me to a dark place that I didn't know was even inside of me. And I thank my family and friends for doing everything in their power to pull me out of the darkness. Shonettda Ball, Daphne Gillespie, Tiffany Gillespie, Titasha Taylor, Clara Jackson, Tyra Lewis, Tonya Ousley, Helen Ousley Tiffany Ousley. I love all of you ladies to the moon and beyond. You all hold a special place in my heart and you have a special role in my life. To my adopted family Crystal Barnett, Shadress Denise, K'wan, Raynesha Pittman, Karoz Norman. I love you all and appreciate your friendship and everything you have ever done for me.

And Special thanks to my Day 1 readers who support anything with my name on it. Mariell Edwards, Rashida McDaniels, Kai-Kai Fisher, Alicia Davis(my cousin) Denise Henson, Lenika Winfield, Terria Miller and Rita King. I love the way you all love my crazy!! I really appreciate all your support.

Words could never truly express the way I'm feeling right now.

My Journey has only just began!! Are you watching?

I am Lincoln Zachariah Donaldson, but I go by Zachariah and my better half goes by the name Lincoln. I come in the name of the Lord. To punish all sinners and to show them the errors in their ways. God's smite will be handed down through me. I am thy wrath, thy rod, and thy vengeance. I will exile all sinners from the world. He that believeth on the Son hath everlasting life. And he that believeth not the Son shall not see life, but the wrath of God abideth on him.

My mother taught me that scripture at the age of five and she never let me forget it. For forgetting it, would be like insulting the Lord and his word and that was definitely not good in my house. The hell I called home, the house that raised me, broke me, built me back up, and turned me into the monster that I am today.

I can still smell the strong odor of urine and blood permeating throughout the house. Every now and then, I can still hear my mother pacing back and forth in a rage yelling my name over and over again. The bites from the insects under the boards in my bedroom where I hid are still stinging me almost 15 years later. I can recite the whole Bible backwards and forwards but there is nothing Godly about me, only evil lurks within the flesh that covers my dark and tortured soul.

1
NIGHT TERRORS

"Lincoln! Lincoln!"

Lincoln heard his mother Dorothy hollering his name as he hid under a few worn down loose boards in his bedroom. He shook feverishly, scared that she might find him. His eyes darted all around the dark hole he'd hid himself in searching for any escape route if need be. However, he knew there was nowhere he could run to if she was to find him. The area was just big enough to fit his tiny frail body into. Tears and snot ran down his face as he tried to make himself small enough to disappear. Lincoln tried his best to keep control of his boney knocking knees, but failed miserably. His heart beat at a rapid speed threatening to break through his chest cavity.

Lincoln listened intently to see how far away Dorothy's footsteps were. He had learned to listen for certain squeaks and other noises on specific boards. At an early age, he had learned survival tactics when it came to his mother. And at that moment, she was standing over his body cursing and yelling obscenities far worse than a drunken sailor. The old wooden boards squeaked under the pressure of her weight with each step she made as dust and spider webs fell down onto his face. He placed his hands over his nose and mouth to keep the dust from going in, not wanting to sneeze, giving up his hiding spot. He knew she would never find him; he had been stuffing himself under the boards for a while, ever since Dorothy's sickness had taken a turn for the worse.

"Lincoln!" she yelled again. "Come on out here, right now, you little bastard, it's time for your repentance! Come pray with ya momma son." She marched back and forth over the boards that Lincoln lay under frozen stiff. He was too scared to breathe, afraid of making even the slightest sound. He could hear the chains to her special homemade whip dragging against the floor. The whip known affectionately across the globe, as The Cat O'Nine Nails was made up of a wooden stick with duct tape going around the base for grip, and coming out of the top were fifteen long barbed wires. It reminded Lincoln of the whip that was used to beat Jesus in the movie "Passion of the Christ." Of course, that was only movie he had ever seen in his young life. No Saturday morning cartoons for him. They had a television but Dorothy said it was full of nothing but the Devil's hidden messages to bring people to him.

"The armies of Satan shall not prevail in my home," is what she used to say to him.

Lincoln knew that once he finally emerged from his hiding spot, she would be furious with him and his punishment would be multiplied by ten. The wrath of God had nothing on his mother when her illness kicked into overdrive. Lincoln had just escaped her grip after she had hit him in the head with an empty plate that was only few minutes before filled with food. He hadn't eaten in days and so he was famished, but she called it Gluttony, and then proceeded to take the plate from him and hit him in the head with it. Before she could get another swing in, he had jumped up and run in to his room.

"He that believeth on the Son hath everlasting life. And he that believeth not the Son shall not see life, but the wrath of God abideth on him," she chanted as she searched Lincoln's bedroom for him.

Lincoln listened as she repeated herself over and over again. That particular scripture meant she was punishing the sinners that day and he wanted no parts of it. He had become accustomed to sleeping under the wooden boards for days without coming out. He would urinate and defecate on himself just to avoid one of her rants. All the little critters of the night hid under the boards with him feasting on his blood, skin, and feces. His body was covered in bites and sores, but to Dorothy, it was the Lord bringing down one of his plagues on Lincoln because of his sins. She had been going strong for about six hours and showed no signs of letting up.

3

"Lincoln! Lincoln come out now!" she screamed. He could hear her throwing things. He didn't have much in his room to begin with, but what little he did have he knew was no longer any good. "Lincoln!"

"Lincoln, man, wake up!" Lincoln's partner Mike yelled as he shook Lincoln from a turbulent slumber.

Lincoln had fallen asleep in the locker room again laying on one of the benches that lined the walls. Mike had gotten used to waking him up from sweaty nightmares because Lincoln rarely went home to sleep. He worked during the night and stayed up for days at a time sometimes. Sleep was the nemesis that Lincoln had yet to concur. He thought about his past every minute of the day, but when he slept, the memories ran through his mind at warp speed. Visions of his mother and her life-sized crucifix taunted what little mental stability he had left.

Lincoln jumped and looked up to see his partner staring down at him with a look of concern written on his face. "I'm up man, I'm up!" He reached up, touched his face, and looked at his hand; it was dripping with sweat. He wiped his hand on his pants and took in a deep breath. He knew one of these days his nightmares were going to give him a heart attack. However, he knew there was nothing that could erase his past.

"You were having one of those damn dreams again, huh?" Mike frowned and walked over to his locker shaking his head. He wished Lincoln would

4

go see someone about his nightmares. Lincoln had already told him about his childhood so he understood where the nightmares where coming from. It had taken years for Lincoln to open up to Mike but once he did, he totally understood why Lincoln was the way he was. Lincoln's mom was crazier than a bag full of cats.

Lincoln rubbed his head in frustration, he wished he could let go of all the memories that invaded his mind every day, but his mother had a strong hold on him. She was killed when he was only ten, but now at the age of 25, he felt her presence more than he did when he was young. She was a torturous lady and took no mercy on him when she felt he needed to be punished.

"I'm about to get in the shower," Lincoln stated as he looked at his watch. It read six thirty so that meant he had about thirty minutes before his nightshift was to start. He liked nightshift because it stopped him from having the night terrors that often plagued his dreams.

"When are you going to get some help about those dreams man?" Mike asked while they drove around looking for something to get into. The nightlife in St. Louis was always live. The city always gave it to you raw and uncut whether you wanted it that way or not. The way the city looked at the present, one would have never guessed that St. Louis once hosted the World's Fair and the Summer Olympics. Downtown St. Louis was now littered with the homeless and prostitutes holding up the walls of the historic buildings standing still as if they were permanent fixtures.

"Look I told you to leave it alone." Lincoln shifted his eyes so he wasn't looking at Mike anymore. He was tired of talking about going to see a psychiatrist. He had been there and done that, but between his mother and Zachariah, he knew no one would ever be able to help him. He had committed horrible sins in the name of the Lord and he knew deep down there was a special place in hell for him. Mike asked him to see someone every time he caught him having nightmares. If Mike only knew that Lincoln was the reaper himself and he was what nightmares are really made of.

How was he supposed to explain to someone that he was the boogeyman and expect them to help him? That shit only happened in the movies and he didn't see any cameras nor production companies around. This was a real life horror story he was living every day of his life. Plus, Lincoln didn't want to go over the story with anyone else, it was bad enough he relived it every day of his life. He had seen a child psychiatrist for a good portion of his childhood and it didn't make a bit of difference. He was forced by the state to see one after his mother's death because of the nature of her death. They wanted to make sure he would be stable enough for adoption and that he wouldn't need to go to a juvenile psychiatric institute. He played the role of a good boy very well, even when he was adopted; he hid his demons from his adopted mother Jill.

"Alright I'm just saying you got that big pretty

house out in the country and never go there. If you don't want it, me and my family of six will gladly switch places with you," Mike joked. He, his wife, and four daughters were living in a four-bedroom home, which seemed to be getting smaller and smaller every day.

"I do go home and them little bad fuckers ain't gon' mess up my damn house," Lincoln laughed.

"Hey those are my little bad fuckers!" Mike knew his kids were terrors on two feet, so he couldn't help but to laugh too.

"I know; they take after you."

They shared a laugh as something on the street caught Lincoln's attention. He could see a transaction going on between a hooker and a John. He knew she was prostitute because of the area they were in and by her wayward attire. The blue shorts were so short and tight that they looked like there were cutting off her circulation. He figured her toes had to be purple, there was no way in the world blood was flowing to them. His 20/20 vision zoomed in on every curve on her body and landed on her pussy print that imitated a baby's fist.

He watched as she put on her best sex strut and approached the car. She leaned into the John's car with her ass sticking out the bottom of her shorts. The seven-inch come fuck me heels made her look statuesque and made every muscle in her legs work overtime. However, she didn't seem to mind, the way she walked in those heels was as if she was born wearing them. Her skin was so dark, that once the streetlight shined down on it, it illuminated the beautiful shimmer of her skin. He didn't make his partner aware of the transaction; he just stored the prostitute's face in his mental rolodex. He knew she was someone that Zachariah would be interested in.

They were making their transaction in front of an abandoned building but he knew she was about to take him to the alley to do some unspeakable acts. No matter how much they tried to breathe life back to the business section of downtown St. Louis, the demons of the night were always there to suck the very life right back out of it. Business activity had improved over time with many new businesses relocating to downtown, but that did nothing, it only brought more victims to the nightwalkers. He shook his head, thinking things would never change no matter how many sinners he got rid of, another just replaced the last one.

"Say, man, did you hear me?" Mike snapped Lincoln out of his inner thoughts.

"Huh, what did you say?" Lincoln looked over to see his partner frowning at him, but he could also see concern in Mike's eyes.

"I said do you want to get something to eat?" Mike was used to him zoning out like that. He would be talking to Lincoln then all of sudden his eyes would start shifting like he was looking at someone or something that wasn't there.

"Yeah my stomach's been growling for a while now, but I know you and the wife are dieting now." He laughed at Mike because Mike's wife was the only one who had been following their diet. Mike was a six-foot tall Caucasian man that looked like he tanned too much and he was a strong two hundred and ninety pounds. His build was thick and he didn't look like he weighed almost three hundred pounds, but once his wife found out how much he weighed, she and the doctor came up with the worst diet in the world for him.

"Aw man to hell with you, I'm trying." The diet his wife had put him on had him hungry every five minutes, so he only stuck to it when he was with her. "Shit, palm-sized portions, no bread, or sugar. You may as well kill me now!" He shook his head.

"Tell your wife to shave that damn unibrow off the middle of your damn forehead. That will shave off about ten pounds by itself. That muthafucka stupid thick!" Lincoln broke into a fit of laughter at Mike's expense.

"My wife loves my unibrow, hater!" Mike was used to Lincoln cracking jokes on him. He didn't mind, the jokes just meant that Lincoln wasn't thinking about the things in his past, at least at that moment.

"A'ight let's get something to eat then."

Lincoln watched from afar, as the prostitute that he had seen earlier got in and out of car after car. She must be good at what she does, he thought because she kept the customers coming. He had dropped his partner off at home for a while after they ate. That had become a routine of theirs over the past few years. Mike liked to check in on his family during the nights they worked and that suited Lincoln just fine. That gave him time to get into his own adventures.

The prostitute leaned up against the abandoned building smoking a cigarette talking to a fellow hooker that looked like she had seen better days. He could tell the other streetwalker was tweaking for a fix by the way she scratched at her arms and squirmed as she leaned against the building. The prostitute he had his eyes set on was very pretty and he wondered what pushed her into the mean streets of St. Louis. He loved the dark shade of chocolate her skin was covered in. Lincoln could tell that if she didn't have the high heels on, she would be very short. Her legs were thick, short, and slightly bowed.

She had traded in her jean shorts for a mini skirt and some fishnet stockings with a tight crop top that stopped just below her breasts since the last time he had seen her. She was the definition of beauty and under different circumstances; he would have loved to get to know her. A love life was forever out of his reach though.

"So put to death the sinful, earthly things lurking within you. Have nothing to do with sexual immorality, impurity, lust, and evil desires,"

Lincoln heard a voice speak into his ear. He gripped the steering wheel and tried squeezing his eyes shut to get the voice out of his head.

"Not tonight, Mother, I'm just looking." He

looked straight ahead staring at the hookers servicing their customers with a phony smile. It seemed as though the night had woken up with a little extra energy. It was live out as if someone had plugged the energy of the night into 1000 volts of electricity. That was the reason he loved working nights, sinners by the dozens, he could just sit back and chose, plucking them off like sitting ducks.

"Those whores don't deserve to live another day, they don't know the Lord our savior son," she explained.

"I know Mother," Lincoln replied frustrated that his mother wouldn't leave him alone. She had been whispering in his ear his whole life about the wayward ways of the world and how sinners needed to be taken off the face of the earth. And like a good son, he always did what his mother asked of him. He gathered the sheep and fed them to the wolf.

"Well act like you know and show these whoremongers the wrath of God dammit!" she yelled.

"Yes Mother."

Lincoln slowly pulled off and crept up slowly on the prostitute he had in his sights. When she saw him coming, she rolled her eyes and began to speed walk down an alley to her right. He followed her into the alley watching her ass jiggle in the tiny, ass hugging skirt she wore. He watched her strut in those heels like she was walking a Victoria's Secret runway. Every other step an ass cheek played peekaboo with him. Once they got deeper into the alley, he got out.

"Hey!" he called to her as he walked towards her. Glass and gravel crumbled under his feet with each step. He scanned the area for any bystanders.

"Look, Officer, I ain't done nothing; you can go on about your business." She waved her hand as she kept her pace steady and fast. She didn't need to get busted that night. It was the one day of the year, she knew she would need to be extra high; and sitting in a jail cell wasn't going to get her right. Her daughter's death hit her hard every day but her heart ached more on the anniversary of day she was taken from her. She shook those thoughts and tried to speed up her pace.

"Please sir just let me go home."

"I said stop!" he yelled and cut her sentence short as he pulled out his stun gun and pointed it at her back. When she kept going, he got a little closer, shot the electrical wires into her body, and he watched her body go stiff as a board and collapse to the ground. Her body locked in an intense shake on the ground. He held the trigger a little longer than he needed to. She couldn't scream because the miniature electrocution she was receiving knocked all comprehension out of her. When he finally let go, she was knocked out and foaming at the mouth. He scooped her up on his shoulder, carried her to his car, popped his trunk, and tossed her in. Lincoln jumped into the police cruiser and sped away.

The whole way to his house, he ground his teeth together; it was a nervous habit he had formed as a child. His heartbeat thumped loudly in his ears. The adrenaline rush he had going was like a high he never wanted to come down from. Lincoln rode in silence as his body led him home, while his mind had gone back down memory lane.

2
THE DEVIL INSIDE

"Lincoln!" Dorothy yelled as she snatched the boards up that he had been lying under. Lincoln was terrified at the sight before him. His mother towered over his small frame with her hair all over the place and her robe hanging open; she wore nothing underneath her robe. Her skin was covered in scratches like she had been trying to claw something out of her. The crazed look in her eyes made him relieve himself of any urine his aching bladder had left in it. She reached in and snatched him out the little hole that he had created in the floor. He was so small she was able to lift him with ease. At the age of seven years old, he couldn't have weighed more than 50 pounds wet with bricks in his pockets.

"Mother, no, please, I'll pray with you!" he screamed as he swung wildly trying to get her to loosen her grip around his neck. He felt his windpipe crushing under the force of her grasp.

"It's too late now sinner." She dropped him and he landed on his feet. Lincoln stood before her crying hysterically and shaking like a leaf blowing in the wind wearing nothing but a pair of tighty-whities. She yanked him by the arm, dragged him into the living room, and pushed him down on his knees in front of her self-made crucifix, a wooden statue that sat in the middle of her bare living room. The only furniture in the room was the life-sized crucifix and an old ratty red carpet that sat in front of it. His mother had moved all the furniture into the basement one day while she was on a rampage in prayer. She said the Lord had told her that the living room was made for prayer only and that she needed to clear out the furniture so she could receive him properly.

Lincoln leaned over and kissed the feet of the statue as he wept silently. Dorothy had told him it was a sin to cry in front of Jesus Christ because he didn't hear the cries of sinners.

"People who conceal their sins will not prosper, but if they confess and turn from them, they will receive mercy," his mother recited as she raised her hand that held her special whip in it, brought it down across Lincoln's back, and snatched it back tearing his flesh from his back. The pain of his skin being ripped from his bones hurt so badly he couldn't even muster enough strength to scream.

"Say it with me sinner!" Dorothy yelled.

Lincoln shook his head to get the memory out of his head as he pulled up to his home. He got out, picked up the prostitute from his trunk, and carried her to the back of his house. He unlocked the door to his shed and dropped her on the floor as he gathered the contraption he had recently ordered online. He had built his own torture chamber in the shed in his backyard after watching a documentary on America's first serial killer. H.H. Holmes.

Lincoln was fascinated with how he had gotten away with having a torture chamber built in the building where he lived and did his work. Lincoln's home was much smaller than Mr. Holmes' was considering his was on the second floor of his building and Lincoln's was a small shed. He was able to build up quite a collection of handmade torture devices but he had only used a few so far. He knew Zachariah had plans to change that very soon.

Once Lincoln got everything set up, he stripped her of all her clothing. He picked her up, lay her across the breeding harness, and strapped her in. He then handcuffed her arms and legs to the base of the harness. Once he was ready, he poured a cup of water over her head.

"Hey what the hell is going on?" The prostitute looked at her handcuffed arms and could see she was strapped to some kind of contraption she had never seen before. Panic immediately set in as she looked around at what looked like a wooden shed she was being held in.

"I am Zachariah and you have been judged. And

it's time for you to pay for your sins," Zachariah stated in a slow monotone voice. He walked around her slowly taking in the sinful beauty that lay before him. Lust consumed him as he thought about gutting her while he deep stroked her into the afterlife.

"What are you talking about? I haven't done anything to you asshole! Let me go!" she yelled as she looked for an escape route.

"It is not my decision, the Lord has spoken. So put to death the sinful, earthly things lurking within you. Have nothing to do with sexual immorality, impurity, lust, and evil desires." Zachariah kneeled down in front of her. "Don't be greedy, for a greedy person is idolater, worshipping the things of this world. Because of these sins, the anger of God is coming."

He shoved a red leather ball that had a strap attached to it deep into her mouth and tightened the straps around her head. He looked down at his watch and knew he didn't have much time left; he needed to get back to Mike. "Your punishment will have to be delayed for a little bit sinner." He ignored her cries and whimpers as he exited the shed and locked the doors.

"Where the hell are you going? Go back and finish what you started you bastard!" Dorothy yelled in his ear.

"Look, bitch, this ain't your sweet little Lincoln you are talking to. If it wasn't for him being attached to you, your ass would have been gone,"

Zachariah gritted as he speed walked to the squad car to get back to Mike in time.

"Zachariah, where the hell did he get your disrespectful ass from? How dare you talk to me that way?"

"Yeah well you should be used to it by now Dorothy. Just like you, I'm here to stay; only I'm here to protect him while you are here to torment him. I'm just waiting on the moment he gets tired of having you around. You were useless then and you are most definitely useless now!

"If he gets rid of me you best believe you're leaving too."

"See now that's where you are wrong, he actually wants me around. Can't say the same for the woman who tried to kill him at the tender age of 10."

Lincoln's mind split the day his mother was killed, and Zachariah only came out when things got too hard for Lincoln to handle. When Lincoln took on his vow to God, Zachariah became a permanent presence in Lincoln's life. At first, only coming out when Lincoln was extremely angry or scared. However, when Lincoln had refused to kill anyone else after his mother made him do an unspeakable act, Zachariah began to play a bigger part in Lincoln's life, taking things to next level.

"We will see about that once I tell him about what you've been doing."

"Isn't this what you and the Lord wanted him to

do? To get rid of all the sinners?" he asked sarcastically.

"Yes but not the way you are doing it. You fucking pervert," Dorothy scoffed at him. "No one told you to stick your deformed devil's rod into these harlots!"

"Yeah well what the fuck ever. If you haven't noticed, it's my way or the highway. You get what you want and I get what I want. Lord knows poor Lincoln ain't getting any action on his own."

"You will rot in hell."

"Yeah right next to your crazy ass now go away." Zachariah reached in his pants pocket and grabbed a loose pill he kept in his pocket for the days he wanted to block their mother out. He stared at the white oval shaped pill for minute before throwing it to the back of his throat and swallowing hard. His mouth was dry from the excitement of what he was going to be doing later on. Zachariah knew it would take a while for the medicine to kick in but that would work out just fine for him. He would be done long before the meds kicked in, he didn't want to leave Lincoln with a mess to clean up.

*****

"Aye you too quiet over there," Mike said as he studied Zachariah not knowing he wasn't looking at Lincoln.

When Zachariah took over, he was always

distant not wanting to give anything away. Zachariah knew he and Lincoln were two totally different people in personality. Where Lincoln still smiled and laughed, Zachariah felt there was no need to do either. Life had dealt Lincoln a flop hand, and put him in no win situations when seen fit. However, unlike Zachariah, Lincoln held hope for a better life when Zachariah knew they were headed to hell in gasoline boxer briefs.

"Oh, I'm good, just people watching." Zachariah was in deep thought about the woman he had in his shed. He would make her beg for her life and repent her sins, but it was already too late in his eyes. The Lord had spoken and she was to pay for her sins. He imagined all the ungodly sinful things she had been doing with her body and mouth to get high or to satisfy a sexual craving. He wondered if sinful nothings slid off her slick tongue and settled in her John's groin. His hands started to itch as he looked at his watch. He had thirty more minutes left on his shift. He impatiently tapped his foot ready to clock out and go home at that very moment.

"You sure you alright?" Mike watched him fidget in his seat. He went from tapping his fingers to his left leg to shifting in his seat like he had ants in his pants. Mike was still getting used to all the little quirks Lincoln showed every day.

"Dude, you worry too much, I'm good." Zachariah put on a fake smile.

"A'ight I don't want no problems out of you."

Lincoln was only five foot eight and Mike stood

a strong six foot three. Even though Lincoln was smaller, Mike knew there was more to Lincoln's innocent baby face features. He knew there was something missing in Lincoln's head, at times it seemed like things just weren't clicking for him. At any given time, he would catch Lincoln talking to himself. Holding real live conversations with himself, sometimes even cursing and yelling at himself. During those times, he stayed away from Lincoln letting him have some space.

"You good fam, what is little ole me going to do to a big feller like yourself?" Zachariah joked making fun of Mike's country accent that slipped out every now and then. He smirked as he looked over at his partner, because he knew that generally everyone around him was deathly afraid of him.

He wasn't the most handsome man in the world, at least in his eyes. He kept his hair cut close to his head, he wasn't bald and it wasn't a czar, his smooth caramel colored skin refused to grow facial hair, and right on his jawline, at his chin, you could see where a chunk of his flesh had been removed. Add all the scars on his body and the zipper looking scar his mother had given him around his neck that didn't make matters any better. He talked with a raspy voice because his mother had damaged his vocal cords when he was younger and that gave him an even more unnerving affect.

"I know the truth, but I'm gon' keep it to myself."

Mike loved his partner; they were like brothers and they had been put together their first day out on their own, and they'd been thick as thieves ever since, but he knew there was something evil lurking around in Lincoln's head.

3
THY WRATH

Zachariah admired his prisoner as she lay asleep uncomfortably strapped to the new contraption that Lincoln had built. If Lincoln didn't get anything else from his mother, he had taken on her building and fix it skills. He could take one look at something and know how to build or make it. Instantly.

The prostitute had perspired so much her dark chocolate skin looked like it had been dipped in honey. The moonlight that seeped in through the cracks in the wooden walls shone just bright enough to give her flesh a sparkling effect. Her ample ass sat up in the air like it was waiting for him to enter it. He walked up to her and placed his hand on her soft ass cheek, walked his fingers up her back, and ran his fingers through her hair. He took a nice amount of her hair into his hand and snatched her head back.

"Wake up sinner, its judgment time," Zachariah sneered. He could see she was trying to say something but it was too late for her to plead her case, the verdict and punishment had already been cast her way. Her body bucked and shook the harness but she was getting nowhere fast.

"Have nothing to do with sexual immorality, impurity, lust, and evil desires. Don't be greedy, for a greedy person is an idolater, worshipping the things of this world. Because of these sins, the anger of God is coming. Do you know that scripture sinner?" Zachariah asked as he pulled out the tools that he would need for their session.

He started out with the same kind of instrument his mom used to beat Lincoln with as a child. He'd made his own version of The Cat O'Nine nails.

Zachariah's version was just a little different from the one his mother had made, it was all metal with thirty-two feet of barbwires hanging from it instead of the fifteen his mother had on hers. When he held it in his hands, he felt sweat beads form all over his body, like a lady going through a menopausal episode. The power he felt towering over her body sent a heat wave through his body, up his spine and back down to the tip of his penis. He took the ball that was strapped in her mouth out and sat it on the ground next to her.

"What is your name sinner?" he asked as he kneeled down in front of her.

"Julia," she cried. This was not the way she

wanted to die. She knew she put herself in danger every day but nothing like this had ever crossed her mind. She looked into the eyes of her captor and could see nothing but evil looking back at her. His dark soul emitted an aura in the atmosphere that vacuumed the air right of the room.

"My name is Zachariah and I am the will of the Lord."

He stood up and loomed over her limp body like a black cloud letting the earth know a storm was brewing, but the atmosphere didn't emit moisture; the air was proving hard to inhale for Julia. Her lungs seemed as though they caught fire as her body temperature rose to an almost unbearable high.

"Please…" She watched every move he made as fear gripped her heart with a vice like grasp. He unbuttoned his shirt and her eyes got as big as saucers at the sight of all the scars on his chest. She began to cry hysterically. "Please, please, I'm sorry."

Her pleas for mercy stopped when he pulled down his pants and boxer briefs. All the blood in her body rushed to her head. His penis hung flaccidly down his leg, the veins in it looked like fat worms under the thin skin, but the scars going up and down his shaft took away from the beauty of such a masterpiece. The horrid sight before her looked like someone had taken a razor and made tic-tac toe boards all over his penis.

"What are you looking at?" Zachariah noticed her eyes lingering on his mangled private parts. The look of disgust that was plastered on her face didn't go unnoticed. She turned a deathly pale. He watched as she dry heaved. The remnants of her earlier meal made its way to the floor in front him, splashing his clothes that lay on the floor.

"No…noth…thing. Please sir just let me go; I won't tell anyone what happened," she begged as emesis ran down her chin onto the old dirty concrete floor.

"I told you your judgment has been made." He stepped completely out of his clothes and flexed his muscles. A tingling sensation had started to run rampant through his body from excitement.

"Who are you to judge me?" she screamed as she finally found her voice.

"I am the will of the Lord and his will shall be done."

He showed no apathy as he walked around to the back of her and got down on his knees. He picked up a jar of Vaseline and rubbed it all over her vagina and ass, and then rubbed it up and down his shaft until it was completely covered. His dick was so hard the head started to hurt a little. The feeling of overwhelming anticipation always took over his senses, making everything on his body beyond sensitive. He massaged her ass cheeks as if he was kneading bread. He pushed both her ass cheeks together, kissed them both softly, and slid his tongue across. He then bit down on her right ass cheek hard, drawing blood. He loved the feel of his teeth breaking through soft flesh.

"The Lord wants you to fuck me, you pervert?" She wanted to scream from the pain of the bite but refused to give him the satisfaction. Zachariah's head snapped up he stared at the back of her head for a moment then went back to what he was doing. He had been getting rid of the whores of St. Louis for years so he'd heard all the insults anyone could throw his way.

After Lincoln's mother Dorothy was killed, she came to him in a dream and told him, that God told her that Lincoln would be the hand that upheld The Lord's will and his will was to send all sinners to be arbitrated and punished.

"The Lord wants you punished for your sins and you will feel the wrath of him throughout this whole lil' scenario." He ran the head of his dick up and down her slit. "Trust me." With clenched teeth, he forced his oversized manhood deep within her tight walls. She screamed out. The pain that erupted in her vagina seemed to touch every nerve ending in her body as he stroked in and out of her. His massive hard on was stretching her insides way pass their limit. He dug his nails into the skin on her back and raked his hands down leaving long scratches that resembled bloody welts. While Julia was in agony, he had reached a sexual high like no other.

Her screams grew louder with each stroke of his death pole. He grunted like an animal in the wild. With every stroke, he went in deeper making all of her female organs burn as if there were flames sitting inside of her. He could feel every muscle in his body contracting with each pump. His body temperature fluctuated between sizzling and freezing.

"Please stop!" Julia pleaded, in all her years of being on the streets, she had never encountered such pain. She had seen all kinds of sick and twisted acts performed, different shaped dicks, even some ugly vaginas, but he took deformed to a whole new level. The thought of his shredded penis inside of her made her want to throw up all over again. She only hoped he would send her to be with her baby girl quickly because she didn't have the strength to end her own life.

Julia took her mind back to when her baby girl died. She had woken up from a three-day binge and found her four-year-old daughter had stuck a needle in her arm; she had shot air into her vein imitating what she has seen her mother doing. Doing this the child caused an air embolism, which is an air bubble trapped in the main bloodstream blocking blood flow to the lungs. Julia saw her baby girl's cold dead body lying on the floor next her and she felt her heart explode. No matter what she was doing out in the streets she loved her daughter with all of her being. Her daughter's dead eyes staring back at her haunted her every day. After that, she fell into a deep depression and felt that she had to be high every minute of the day and would do anything to stay high and not face her reality. Because her reality showed that, she had failed miserably as a mother and as a human being. What kind of mother would even put her child in that type of situation? A sense of causalgia plagued her every day of her life, a pain that wasn't physical but she felt an intense pain in her soul every time she thought about her daughter.

"Shut up whore!" He watched his dick going in and out her and smiled when he saw the blood starting to run down his thighs. He felt an electrical current surge throughout his entire body as he reached his peek. "Grrrrrrrrrrr," he growled as he shot his seeds deep into her tortured hot box. He panted for a minute as he pulled out and squeezed the last of his seed on her back.

She whimpered as she felt him getting up from behind her. She prayed that was end. At this point, she wanted him to take her out her misery.

"Are you ready to repent and ask the Lord for his forgiveness?" Zachariah asked as he looked down on her body with his special whip in hand.

"Repent for what? Why are you doing this, you sick fuck?" Julia no longer felt the need to beg anymore. She welcomed death with open arms at this point. Zachariah had taken the last piece of her soul she had left.

"Such a filthy mouth, but I'll fix that later, it your body's turn for punishment." He raised his hand and brought the whip down hard on her ass making sure the little spikes in the barbwire stuck in her skin before he snatched it back ripping the flesh from her body. The screams that resonated throughout the shed whispered a sweet melody to his soul.

"Repent sinner!" Zachariah raised the whip, tightening his grip and towering over her as he regarded her filthy flesh, disgusted by the sins; he knew she had committed. He released the whip with such anger it tore through her skin exposing white meat.

"I haven't done anything!" The pain was becoming unbearable. The stench of blood and torn flesh filled the room but that didn't stop Zachariah from whipping her with the expertise of a slave master. She couldn't see her back but from the searing pain, it felt like she was being skinned alive.

"Repent sinner!" he roared as he brought the whip down again.

"Father God, please stop this!"

"He sent me; he no longer hears your sin filled pleas."

"God, you said you would protect the meek. The ignorant! I am still your child!" Julia pleaded.

"If we confess our sins, he is faithful and just and will forgive us our sins and purify us from all unrighteousness." Julia lowered her head in shame but Zachariah was not satisfied. He grabbed her neck and lifted her head so they were looking into each other's eyes. The terror in his eyes made her tremble.

"Confess your sins to the Lord!" Zachariah shouted.

She cried finally saying it out loud. "Father forgive me I have sinned. I'm sorry I killed my child, father; please forgive me. I killed my child...I killed my child!" She had never admitted her part in her daughter's death. Her confessions cut deeper than Zachariah's whip.

"My father, your Lord and savior always forgives the sins of his children. But you must suffer for the wrongs you've committed against others." Zachariah beat her until the walls were painted in flesh. He stepped back and regarded his handiwork. Her body lay wilting...beat. He beat her into exhaustion but the rise and fall of her chest indicated that she still breathed life.

He stood naked covered in blood with a sense of power surging through his veins. He then bowed his head in prayer.

"But the fearful, and unbelieving, and the abominable, and murders, and whoremongers, and sorcerers, and idolaters and all liars, shall have their part in the lake which burneth with fire and brimstone."

4
IN THE BEGINNING

"Lincoln dinner is ready!"

Lincoln heard his mother Dorothy call from the kitchen. He had been held up in his room for days, worrying every moment of each day about when she was going to decide he was her son again. The fumes coming from his body would have been revolting to anyone with a sense of smell, but he had grown used to not bathing for days at a time.

When Dorothy's mind checked out, there was no bathing or eating for either of them. He barely got a chance to use the actual bathroom for fear of running into her in the hallway. He often found himself urinating and defecating in the corner of his room or under the boards where he hid from his mother.

"Ok Mother." Lincoln smiled and breathed a

sigh of relief because he knew she was her normal self that day. In his seven years on earth, he had learned how to read the atmosphere and put out feelers to see if he was going to have a decent or turbulent day. On the days she cooked, he was a happy little boy because everything felt normal. Dorothy would go through spurts of not knowing what reality was and making him starve for days on end. He would be so hungry that his body would ach for hours. The hunger pains would be so unbearable that he would eat his own feces. When his mother would come out of her mental vacations, she never remembered anything that had happened. She was loving and affectionate towards Lincoln.

When Lincoln walked into the kitchen, he stopped and admired Dorothy's beauty. Her skin was the perfect shade of honeydew, her long beautiful brown curly locks hung down her back with not a hair out of place. Her facial features mirrored his with her high cheeks bones, thick lips, and bushy eyebrows. She wore a pair of beige slacks and a pink button up shirt. She finished the outfit with a pair tan and pink wedges.

Lincoln could remember a time when his mother kept her appearance up every day. She wouldn't dare let anyone see her without her face made up or hair not combed to perfection. However, days like this had become rare, far and few between.

"Good morning Mother," Lincoln said as he slid into the chair furthest away from her. He knew that at any moment, she was liable to flip out for no reason at all. He had learned that the hard way one day. She was hugging him and telling him she loved him and after she finished the sentence, she commenced to try to choke the life out of him, screaming that he was a sinner that came to take her life. So he made sure to keep a good safe distance from her at all times.

"Good morning baby." She walked up to him to give him a kiss on the forehead and he jumped. She very rarely got that close to him anymore unless they were kneeling down in prayer together or she was beating him just for breathing.

"I'm sorry." He put his head down. On days like these, he would always be confused on what to do. On one hand he craved his mother's love but on the other hand he was deathly afraid of her.

"Hush my child, it's ok." She smiled at him. He looked up and smiled back at her. She sat the plate of food in front of him; she had cooked his favorite meal. Chilidogs. His stomach growled at the sight of the food in front of him. The aroma of the food wafted through all his senses and settled at the bottom of his stomach. He hadn't eaten in two days, he was happy she had come out of her mental vacation early this time. He didn't know if his little body would be able to take another day. The hunger pains were starting to wreak havoc on his body. She had told him on many occasions, that not eating was like fasting for God and sinners needed to cleanse their soul before they could talk to the Lord. However, he couldn't remember for the life of him what sin he committed to have to go without food so much.

No one around knew what Lincoln was going through because he didn't attend school, no one even knew she had a child in the house with her. Dorothy homeschooled him. His study consisted mainly of math and the Bible. She had Lincoln out of wedlock, her family disowned her, and Lincoln's married father wanted no parts of them. Dorothy thought she was in love but found out he was married a few months before Lincoln was born. She was heartbroken and never quite the same again. She had given up everything for Lincoln's father, and all he had given her was a bunch of broken promises then left her alone to raise their son all by herself.

Lincoln gobbled his food down before she could change her mind. As he was wiping his mouth, he felt a pain strike through the back of his head. He fell to the floor, reached for the back of his head, and saw blood on his hand. When he looked up, Dorothy was towering over him with a familiar deranged look in her eyes. He could barely see her as dots dancing around in front of his eyes, but he could recognize that stance a mile away.

"Who told you to eat sinner? You didn't finish your fasting."

"You did Mother," he cried as pain radiated down the back of his neck. He tried to inch away before she could get close again. He knew he shouldn't have let his guard down, but he loved his mother no matter what she did to him and his little heart craved her affection and love.

"I ain't told you shit!" she yelled as she snatched

him up in the air. He was a tiny seven-year-old, due to lack of nutrition, so it was nothing for her to pick him up by his neck. "You are supposed to be fasting for the Lord's forgiveness, sinner!" she yelled as she threw him across the kitchen. His head landed on the wall. He shook his head, jumped up, and ran to his room to get into his hiding spot. She gave chase and caught him before he could hide and dragged him into the living where her statue of Jesus Christ sat.

"Mother please it's me!" he cried, but she had already snapped out. "Mother it's me Lincoln!" he screamed as he scratched at her hands.

"My child is no sinner you must repent. Pray with me child." She pushed him down on his knees.

"Repent ye, therefore and be converted that your sins may be blotted out, when times of refreshing shall come from the presence of the Lord. Say it!" she yelled

"I don't know that one Mother." His little body shook in terror. There was something new in the air and he didn't know what was going to happen next. She kept a firm grip on his hair making it feel like his scalp was being ripped off. At his young age, he knew a good portion of the Bible. That's what he and his mother did every day, at least when he wasn't hiding from her, even then, he still listened as she read the Bible out loud.

"Only sinners don't know the Bible and you must be punished," she said calmly as she pushed his head to the feet of the statue. "Kiss his feet and beg for forgiveness." Lincoln cried as he grabbed a hold of the base of the statue and kissed the feet. He didn't see her going to retrieve her special whip. She'd made it one day in one her psychotic breaks when she couldn't find Lincoln. "The Lord doesn't answer sinners." She raised her hand and swung the whip with all her might. Once she felt it latch onto his skin, she yanked it back making the flesh from his bones fly everywhere as it was ripped from his body. Surprised by the pain that rocked his body, Lincoln screamed out in pain.

"Mother why, why, why?" he shrieked.

"You are a sinner and you must be punished." She charged towards him as he scurried to the nearest corner of the room. He was terrified. He had backed himself up into a corner and had nowhere to go.

"I'm your son stop!" He bawled uncontrollably, his back felt like fire was sitting on it. "Mother stop please," he pleaded on deaf ears, he could see his loving mother had gone away and the woman who tormented him on a daily basis had checked in.

"I'll stop when the Lord tells me your punishment is over." She swung the whip again not caring where the barbwires planted themselves. A few landed on his arms and chest, two caught onto the skin of his chin and cheek. She snatched her hand back tearing flesh from his body once again.

"Mother please!" Lincoln screamed. He was in so much agony he couldn't even scream out anymore. Exhaustion was trying to consume him but instead of trying to force his lungs to work, in a last ditch effort, he got up and darted to his room making it to his hiding spot. He could hear her footsteps speeding toward his room. He put his hands over his mouth to make sure she couldn't hear him.

"Lincoln!" she screamed as she pulled at her own hair. "Lincoln!"

He jumped every time she screamed his name. He knew this would be one of those times where he would be under those wooden beams for a while and he was grateful he had gotten a meal this time.

"Yea though I walk through the valley of shadow of death, I will fear no evil for thou art with me thy rod and thy staff they comfort me," he said a small prayer for himself. He got comfortable with his night crawlers and played the waiting game of how long she would be on vacation this time around.

5
MY SAVING GRACE

"Hi my name is Gabrielle Tymes and I would like to make a report." A pretty young lady that looked like she had seen better days smiled at Lincoln. He could see bruises on her face that had begun to turn yellow indicating they were healing and he could also see bruises that were dark purple letting him further know she had been recently beaten.

"Yes ma'am, I'm Officer Donaldson can you tell me what happened?" he asked looking at the woman standing in front him as if he was awestruck.

She looked disheveled with her hair pulled back into a sloppy ponytail, giving full view of her bruises and bite marks on her neck and face. With all bruising, he could still see the beauty in her. She was on the thick side, a little short, but her smile was what caught Lincoln's eye. She genuinely smiled at him. He liked the fact that through her pain she was still able to find a reason to smile. His scars didn't make her stomach turn like so many other people. He knew the look of repulsion all too well and hated when he received it before anyone got a chance to know him.

"Um…is there a woman I can talk to?" Gabrielle looked down to the floor, too ashamed to talk to him about what had happened to her. She figured a woman would be more understanding of her plight.

"Are you sure, it's no problem for me to help you." Lincoln was almost pleading for her to let him help her. He was used to being around hardened criminals and sinners, but she was something different. The moment he saw her, he knew she was sent to him for a reason. Her presence calmed his soul and all she was doing was smiling at him.

"Can we go somewhere private?" She looked around the busy police stations. There was criminals handcuffed to benches, women with kids who she guessed were waiting for their baby fathers to get released. She unconsciously adjusted her coat to pull it further up around her neck, feeling like everyone could read her broken spirit through her clothes.

"Follow me." Lincoln led the way to a back office. He wanted to be around her for some reason. No woman had ever had such an effect on him. He took a look back at her as they walked and noticed more bruises around her neck. At that angle, he could see the hand print that made its home around her neck. He turned his head quickly. He didn't want her to be so uncomfortable that she wouldn't be able to talk to him. He knew how it made him feel when people stared at his scars. When people gawked at him, it made him feel insecure and self-conscious. He often wore long-sleeved collared shirts to hide all the war wounds his mother had left him with.

"Have a seat," Lincoln said as he pointed to a chair across from him and he sat down at the iron desk. She nervously sat, taking in her surroundings. The gray cracking paint that covered the walls gave the room an ominous look. The only furniture in the room was the steel desk she sat at and the two chairs that she and Lincoln where sitting in. She looked over at the two-way mirror and wondered who was on the other side of the glass. Were they waiting for her to tell her story for them to go gossip and tell everyone what had been happening to her? Were they going to laugh at how pitiful her life was? Were they going to judge her situation? Before she met her husband, she had always laughed at the women who stayed with an abusive husband and wondered what made them stay.

"Would you like something to drink before we start?" he asked as he pulled out his pen and pad to take notes.

"No sir." She removed her coat and began to nervously fidget with nonexistent dust on the desk. She kept her eyes locked on the desk in front of her too afraid to look up and see the pity in his eyes.

"Whenever you are ready." He looked her over

and his soul was set on fire at all the bruises he saw on her body. Her light complexion was covered in yellow, green, and purple bruises. The bruises told a story, that whenever whoever was beating on her thought she was healing, he wanted to break her again. Lincoln wanted to hold her to make her feel safe and let her know he would protect her. He turned his head for a moment when she started crying before she even started talking. He handed her a box of tissues that he pulled from a drawer under the desk.

"Thank you, I'm sorry, I must look a mess." She chuckled as she pushed her wild hair strands back into the sloppy ponytail she threw at the top of her head. "Well I'm here to report my abusive husband. He's been beating me for years and I can't take it anymore." She took a deep breath and Lincoln dug his pen into his thigh to keep his anger in check. "I really think he is going to kill me one day, I don't have anywhere to go. So I'm hoping you all will help get him away from me."

"Are you willing to press charges?" Lincoln questioned.

"Yes that's why I'm here!" she got an attitude.

"Well ma'am we get a lot of women in here that say they are willing to press charges but when the time comes, they recant their story." He searched her eyes for sincerity to see if she would really go through with it. To see if she really was through with him and wanted him gone.

"Well I'm ready to go through with it. He is a

real sicko! What kind of husband rapes his wife?"
She shook her head as tears began to flood her eyes.
"He beats me because I can't have kids, when it's
his fault that I keep losing them." With every word,
the tears threatened to choke her making it even
harder for her to breathe, it felt like the oxygen in
the room had been sucked out. "He has caused five
miscarriages by beating me while I was pregnant.
My left arm has been broken; both my eyes have
been swollen shut numerous times and I can't even
count how many of my ribs are still in their natural
position. So, Mr. Officer, I am definitely ready for
him to just die, if I can't get that I will settle for jail,
where someone will rape him every night. That
would do just fine."

The more she talked the more Lincoln felt drawn
to her. He didn't know if it was because of her
abuse story or the fact there was someone in the
world the he could actually feel sorry for.

"We will need to take pictures of any bruises you
may have. I'll send in a female officer to take the
photographs. I'm not going to promise an
immediate response because abuse is one of the
hardest charges to make stick, especially if you
don't have a history on record." He could see the
look of defeat on her face. "But you came to the
right person. I'm going to do my best to make sure
he is never able to hurt you again," he declared
already making up in his head what he would do to
the woman beater. Normally, he only made women
suffer for their sins, but he didn't mind trying it on a
man. Men were just as bad as women were and

some of them needed to be taught a lesson too. "I will need all of his information and do you think you will be able to go stay with someone for a while?"

"I don't have any family or friends here, nor do I have any money to go anywhere." She began to cry again feeling overwhelmed.

"That's ok; we have a fund here for women in need of emergency assistance." He thought of a quick lie, he would help her any way he could. He had plenty of money saved up since he never did anything nor did he shop. The money he did spend went towards food and what bills he had. He had no rent because when he became of age he had inherited his childhood home and fixed it up. His foster mother begged him not go back there, but he was drawn to the house and couldn't let it go.

"Really? I've never heard of a fund for abused women." She gave him a questioning look.

"It's something new. You fill out this paperwork and I'll get you the funds for a hotel room you can use for a week."

"Well what will I do after the week is up?" She looked up at him.

"We will worry about that when the time comes. But something tells me you will be back in your home safely without any worries."

"Hey what is up with you dude?" Mike nudged Lincoln as they drove around waiting on some criminal activity to happen.

"I'm good. Just thinking about that lady that came in today. She told me her story and I didn't think I would ever have the right to feel sorry for anyone, but damn she got me feeling some type of way." He blew out an exaggerated breath.

"Damn she must've been drug through the mud in order for you to get ya feelings in an uproar. What happened? I saw you walk her into an office. Did she press charges?"

"Yeah she pressed charges. Not that it will do any good." He shook his head knowing the system didn't have any room for a battered woman's complaints.

"What you want to creep on him? You know we can make him disappear!" Mike laughed but Lincoln didn't. He had actually hit the nail on the head with his comment. Lincoln had every intention of making him pay for his abuse of Gabrielle. No woman deserved to be treated that way. He would torture a man for days if they ever put their hands on his mother Jill.

"No need, God don't like ugly, he will get his. I told his wife to find somewhere to stay until we could get him away from her." Every time Lincoln closed his eyes, he saw her bruises instead of seeing the constant nightmare that played on repeat twenty-four hours a day in his memory bank, and he didn't know how he felt about that. Normally, he would leave this type of work for Zachariah, but this was personal to him.

Lincoln couldn't wait for his shift to be over. After he had given Gabrielle enough money for a hotel room for a week, he put his plan into motion. He never put the paperwork into the system. He simply took it all with him and went home to gather a few things. Plus, he knew he would need to change out of his uniform. He headed to Gabrielle's home where her husband would be. Lincoln would make him pay dearly for mistreating his wife.

It was still early in the morning so Lincoln hoped that the husband would be asleep or just going to sleep. From the information Gabrielle had given him, her husband worked night shift. That's how she was able to get away during the night to file a report against him. He pulled up to the house and looked around the neighborhood to see if he could see any nosey neighbors. From the outside looking in, you would have thought a happy family lived in the house, but from what he had been told, he knew that was far from the truth. He pulled down the street so no one would be looking at a suspicious car parked outside of their home.

He got out and causally walked up to the back of the house, pulled out a Slim Jim, and jammed it between the lock on the door and the frame. The door creaked open and Lincoln peeked his head inside to see if anyone was around. His heart beat a thousand pumps per minute and his hands began to sweat. Thoughts of what he was about to do brought his anxiety up ten levels. He froze when he thought he heard something moving behind him. He slowly turned to see the door was still open. He breathed a sigh of relief and continued on his way through the house. He peeked in door after door until he found her husband sleeping, snoring loudly; naked as the day he was born. He seemed not to have a care in the world. However, Lincoln was about to change all that. He hadn't killed in years and he didn't know what was propelling him forward to go through with it.

Lincoln pushed the door all the way open, pausing when he heard it creak. He slipped in, crept to the side of the bed, and loomed over his resting body. He pulled out the Billy club he had brought in from his car as a last minute thought. The husband slept peacefully on his stomach just the way Lincoln wanted him. He raised the Billy club in the air and brought it down on the spot where his head ended and spine began, knocking him out cold. The husband never knew what happened.

Once Lincoln got the husband situated how he wanted him, he began. He tapped the husband on the shoulder, but he didn't budge so Lincoln pulled out the cattle prod he had amongst the toys he brought. He flipped the switch and placed the tip of it on the husband's ass cheek. The husband jumped and screamed out loud, but he couldn't move; he looked around frantically trying to see what was going on, it felt like a dog had just bitten him on his ass.

"Hey man what the hell is going on?" he yelled as he fought against his restraints. He was handcuffed to the base of the bed on his stomach.

"Today is judgment day," Lincoln calmly stated.

"The fuck are you talking about? Get these things off me!" he yelled as he twisted his neck trying to see Lincoln standing behind him.

"But the fearful, and unbelieving, and the abominable, and murders, and whoremongers, and sorcerers, and idolaters and all liars, shall have their part in the lake which burneth with fire and brimstone. It is time for you to repent."

"Repent? What kind of crazy mess is going on? Where is my wife?" He kept twisting his head left and right to see if he could get a good look at Lincoln.

"She is safely tucked away; you will never see her again or put your hands on her again." Lincoln ran the cattle prod up his legs. "What is your name sinner?"

"Greg…What are you doing?" he stuttered as panic had taken over his senses at the mention of his wife and putting his hands on her. He knew he was wrong for the way he treated her, but it was all he knew. His father did it to his mother his whole life and he was never taught that it was wrong to beat women. His mother never left his father so he thought it was something that was supposed to happen to keep them home.

"Greg I am the will of the Lord and I have been sent here to place his wrath upon you. You have been judged and your punishment has been set." Lincoln pulled out his special whip and he swung it hard making sure that every spike on the wires of the whip stuck into to Greg's skin before he yanked it back. Blood, skin, and chunks of meat splashed on Lincoln's face and clothes. Lincoln felt a special kind of tingle go down his spine that he hadn't felt in years.

"Ahhhhhhh!" Greg screamed out. "Please stop, I won't…" Lincoln swung it again making the wires attach to back of his thighs and pulled back again with all his might making skin and flesh splatter all over the place. Lincoln beat Greg until the back of his body looked like an uncooked pizza.

"Are you ready to repent sinner?" Lincoln asked as he ran the cattle prod up Greg's leg and stopped once he had gotten to his anus.

"Wait…wa…ait ple…ase!" His sentence got caught in his throat when he felt a small object slide into his anus. "Wait please, God, no! I'm sorry! Tell her I'm sorry and she is free to go." Greg tried to squeeze his colon muscles tight to push the object out. "God please!

"God is no longer here. He doesn't hear the prayers of sinners." Lincoln turned the cattle prod back on as it sat in Greg's asshole and let it sit in there until his body stopped twitching.

"He that believeth on the Son hath everlasting life, and he that believeth not in the Son shall not see life; but the wrath of God abideth on him." Lincoln prayed over Greg's corpse. He pulled out a small can of gasoline he had in his bag of goodies and poured it all over the bed and floor until he was back at the back door. He pulled out a pack of matches, lit them, then tossed them into the gasoline and watched as the line of gasoline caught fire. He waited for a second until he heard the whooshing sound of fire whisper into the air.

6
MONSTER IN THE MAKING

"Mother, no please, I'll pray with you!" Lincoln screamed.

"It's too late now sinner."

Lincoln stood before his mother crying hysterically and shaking like a leaf blowing in the wind. She yanked him by the arm, dragged him into the living room, and pushed him down on his knees in front of her self-made crucifix. Lincoln leaned over and kissed the feet of the statue as he wept silently. His mother thought it was a sin to cry in front of Jesus Christ because he didn't hear the cries of sinners.

"People who conceal their sins will not prosper, but if they confess and turn from them, they will receive mercy," his mother recited as she raised her hand that held her special whip in it and brought it down across Lincoln's back. She snatched it back ripping his flesh from his back. It hurt so much he couldn't even scream.

"Say it with me sinner!" she yelled as he rolled around on the floor in pain trying to reach his back. She hadn't used her special whip on him in years because he had gotten good at hiding, but now that he had been found, he didn't know if he would be alive after that day. Dorothy raised her arm again, brought the whip down on his flesh and pulled back over and over again until he was lying there almost lifeless. She breathed like a raging bull as she watched her only son lay on the floor covered in blood not moving. Realization hadn't set in that it was her son, her only child, laying on the floor near death. Lincoln heard her walking away and he slowly turned his head to the statue with tears in his eyes.

The pain was so unbearable he prayed for death to come. "Please God make it stop." He cast his eyes back down to the floor and saw a chisel his mother had been using on the statue. She worked on the statue for years making sure she had every nook and cranny of it as perfect as it could possible get. Slowly he reached for it and slid it under him.

Dorothy calmly walked to the kitchen, got a butcher knife out of the drawer, and walked back over to Lincoln. She pulled his frail, limp body that was covered in blood up into her lap. "For God so loved the world, that he gave his only begotten son, whosoever believeth in him should not perish, but have everlasting life." Tears ran down her face as she prepared to sacrifice her only son for the Lord's will. She could see evil in her son every time she looked into his eyes. She knew that one day; he would become the very thing she prayed against. He would be a killer, a rapist, and a liar, a sinner of all sinners and she wanted to stop it before he transformed.

Lincoln gripped the chisel he held tightly in his hand as he felt her slide the cold steel up to his neck. "Lord please bless his soul," she cried as she began to slide the knife from one end of his neck to the other. However, before she could finish, Lincoln brought the chisel up and stabbed it into her ear with all the power his body had left. A look of shock covered her face as she fell backwards. Lincoln fell on the floor on the side of her bleeding profusely from his neck. She had gotten more than halfway across before he stopped her. Both lay staring into each other's eyes as the life faded from Dorothy's eyes. The last thing she thought was, Lord forgive him, before she took her last breath. Lincoln cried as he watched his mother die from his actions. The last thing he remembered was hearing the front door being busted open and everything faded to black.

When Lincoln awoke, he was in a hospital laying on his stomach covered in bandages. He tried to move his body and he felt a searing pain shooting all over his body.

"Please sweetie, don't move too much," he heard a gentle voice whisper to him. He couldn't turn his neck so he waited for them to come into his view.

"You are in the hospital honey. My name is Jill Reynolds and I'm your nurse." She kneeled down in front of him so she was looking at him in the eyes. Her heart broke every time she looked at him. She could tell he had been through a lot during the short time he had been on earth.

"Wha..." Lincoln tried to ask a question but the scorching sensation in his throat stopped him.

"Don't speak, get you some rest I'm here with you sweetie." The nurse had been sitting with him since the day they had brought him in. Lincoln was lucky that there happened to be a couple of joggers running in the woods, that morning his mother decided it was time for him to die. Their house sat at the top of a hill in the woods, it wasn't a creepy looking home, just very private. The joggers heard his screams and her yelling and called the police immediately.

Jill had been a nurse for almost thirty years and never had she seen such heartlessness. When they turned his body over, she broke out into a fit of tears. Almost all the flesh on his body had been ripped from his bones. He was so tiny you would have never thought he was ten years old; he resembled a really sick six-year-old boy. The sight of him tugged at her heartstrings something awful and she vowed to take care of him until he was back in good health.

Jill ended up adopting Lincoln and did her best to make him feel loved, but his past haunted him so terribly that he was too afraid to let anyone get near him. If his own mother could try to kill him, there was no telling, what someone else would do to him. She never gave up on him though; she showered him with love. Even when people would come knocking at her door, saying that he was sociopath, and they thought he was killing all the neighborhood animals.

Lincoln would cry and blame everyone else for not liking him and pleaded that it wasn't him. But secretly, he had been trapping and killing squirrels, rabbits, the lapdogs that roamed into their yard, and the cats. He would skin them, gut them, then burry them in his backyard.

Jill knew deep down inside as she watched him over the years that he was damaged, but she just wasn't ready to give up on him.

Though the first few years where difficult, he had come a long way compared to the day she brought him home. At first, she would find him sleeping in the closet or under his bed. He would take food out of the cabinets and refrigerator and hide it in his room. He was so used to having his food taken from him that he was making sure that he kept some hidden in case she decided he couldn't eat. They went to a child psychiatrist but he wouldn't open up to them. He basically stayed mute and didn't try to make any friends.

He and Jill grew very close considering they were all each other had. Lincoln loved her as best as his damaged heart knew how. On his eighteenth birthday, he inherited the home he grew up in and a trust fund that even he didn't know about. As far back as he could remember, his mother never worked and he never knew why, never questioned it. Her parents disowned her but still paid all her bills and put a trust fund up for him for when he turned eighteen. He moved out and back into his childhood home against the wishes of Jill. No matter what people thought of him, she loved him dearly and would be lonely without him around. But she let him go; she knew it was what he wanted. She truly saw him as her son and not the evil child that everyone tried to paint him as, her blinders were pulled all the way down, and her heart wouldn't let her see the evil lurking in his eyes.

The first time Lincoln walked into his home, he laid in the spot where his mother died for hours, crying. It looked the same way it had the day he killed her. He stared at the crucifix that his mother had made and crawled over to it and kneeled in front of it. An overwhelming feeling washed over him like a tsunami drowning him. There was a thick feeling of dread that threatened to choke the life out of him, but at the same time, a sense of peace washed over him, because he was home.

"So put to death the sinful, earthly things lurking within you. Have nothing to do with sexual immorality, impurity, lust, and evil desires. Don't be greedy, for a greedy person is an idolater, worshiping thing of this world. Because of these sins, the anger of God is coming," his mother's sweet voice whispered in his ear reciting her favorite scripture. He kept his head in a bowed position as he let the words spin around in his head. No matter what transpired between them, he loved his mother at one point. She was all he had.

"I've been waiting for you to come home. My child it's time for you do what the Lord saved you for. Your calling is upon you."

He looked around because it felt like his mother was sitting on the side of him. He had been hearing his mother's words for years but never had he felt her presence so strongly before. He turned and saw his mother kneeled down next to him.

"Mother," he whispered. "I've missed you," he confessed.

"Yes my child its time. The Lord told me, you are to be his will and show the sinners of the world his wrath. Are you prepared for your mission in life my child?" His mother never looked his way. She kept her head facing the crucifix. Her eyes roamed the length of the statue as if she was admiring Jesus Christ in the flesh, as if she could see something that Lincoln couldn't.

"Yes, Mother, I am ready. I am the will of the Lord and his will shall be done."

7
HAUNTED SOUL

"Hey man did you hear about that big fire that happened this morning?" Mike asked Lincoln as they prepared for their shift to begin.

"No, when was it?" Lincoln feigned ignorance.

"Humph," Mike looked at his partner curiously, wondering if he had anything to do with what happened. He didn't know why, but he would bet his last dollar that Lincoln had something to with what happened at that house. "Funny thing is it was the husband of that lady that came in and filed a complaint." Mike had seen the paperwork sitting on Lincoln's desk.

"Damn, really, that's fucked up. Maybe it was his turn to pay for his sins." Lincoln shrugged his shoulders and went about putting the finishing touching on his uniform.

"Another funny thing, I never saw the report put into the system that she filed." He didn't want to come out and ask because he didn't know what type of bag Lincoln would come out of.

"What are you getting at man? Spit it out." Lincoln turned to look at Mike and could see he wanted to say something but was afraid.

"Did you do it?" Mike held his breath waiting for whatever answer or reaction he was about to receive.

"Nope." Lincoln didn't feel the need to elaborate on his answer. All Mike needed to know was he didn't do it.

"Ok, man, I was just asking, don't pay me no mind." Mike laughed the situation off, but felt deep down inside his partner had just lied to him. "You think the wife had something to do with it?"

"She didn't come off as a killer to me, so I don't know."

"Man I wouldn't put nothing past a woman when she is pissed." They laughed at Mike's joke.

"Yeah, you right. You should know."

"Aw man, fuck you. My wife is very happy!" Mike laughed because Lincoln was giving him the yeah alright look. His wife had been at him about his work hours before they came up with the plan of him going home at night during their shift. For now, she was content.

*****

"Excuse me is Officer Donaldson in?" Lincoln heard someone ask as he and Mike were walking out of the locker room. Lincoln looked to where the question had been asked, saw Gabrielle standing there, and his heart skipped a beat. He was happy to see her and fought within himself to hide the smile that was trying to spread across his face.

"Yes ma'am how may I help you? Is there something I forgot to do?" He walked up to her with Mike on his heels.

"Um, no sir. I just wanted to talk to you for a minute." Once again, she found herself looking around the police station feeling uncomfortable. Unconsciously, she adjusted the collar of her shirt.

"Sure follow me. I'll be right back," he turned to Mike."

"I just wanted thank you for what you did." She looked at Lincoln and admired him. She didn't see any scars when she looked at him, only a handsome gentleman whom had helped her in her time of desperate need.

"Excuse me, what did I do?" He gave her perplexed look. Lincoln knew what she was talking about but he would never admit it.

"My husband, he's dead." Gabrielle returned the perplexed look Lincoln had just given her. She prayed he was the one who had helped her out. She needed it to be him. She had already painted him as her savior and she would be forever in his debt. The moment she found out her husband was dead; she felt an overwhelming love for the man standing before her. No matter what he said, she felt it in her soul that it was him.

"I'm sorry for your loss," he began.

"Don't bother with that statement. Because I damn sure am not sorry." She took in a deep breath. "Look I know you can't admit it, but I thank you from the bottom of my heart." She searched his eyes for answers but got none. His face held a blank expression. "Give me a call or come and visit me. I have a week left at the hotel." She patted him on the chest as she walked past him.

When Lincoln felt her hand on his chest, his body felt a warm sensation travel through his veins. He stood there in a trance until he felt a firm hand land on his shoulder.

"Looks like someone has been bitten by the love bug," Mike teased. He honestly didn't care how Lincoln met the woman. If she could bring even the tiniest piece of happiness to Lincoln's life, he would accept her.

"Really, where did that come from? She just needed to add some info to her report."

"For what, ain't he dead?" Mike laughed. "Ok I digress, whatever man. You want to stay in denial, that's fine by me." He threw his hands up in surrender.

"You ready to go to work?" Lincoln wanted to change the subject. He wondered how they knew that it was he that had killed her husband. Was he that transparent? He and Zachariah had been killing for years and no one had ever looked at him. At the thought of killing, Julia popped into his head and the fact she was still out in his shed. Zachariah had never kept a victim so he had totally forgotten about her being back there. He would check on her after his shift and hopefully, Zachariah would finish her off.

"This shit is just sad. All these women have been reduced to nothing but open legs, junkies, and piss pots." Mike shook his head as they rode down a dark street of downtown St. Louis. The street was once known for its high-end shopping boutiques and restaurants. Now it had been reduced to nothing more than a whore's stomping grounds. Liquor bottle, needles, condom wrappers, and other what not's littered the street making it look like an outside crack house. Everyone walked around looking like the walking dead as some leaned against the buildings and nodded off from whatever their drug of choice was and others scanned the block looking for a victim who was stupid enough to come waltzing through their neck of the woods.

"I know; all of them need to be sterilized then hung publicly," Lincoln declared drawing a strange look from Mike.

"Damn really, some of them just fell on hard times and need help getting back on track." Mike shook his head at Lincoln's harshness.

"Yeah, that is true, but some of them love what they do." He watched as the whores mingled and car hopped; his eyes locked in on one particular lady. She stood taller than the others did, her face looked strong, and her shoulders were broad. Lincoln knew she was a transvestite, the ultimate sinner in his eyes. To him people who deceived others under those kind of false pretenses were the worst. He would surely be back for the he/she.

"I guess, but anyway, what you gonna do about ole girl?"

"What do you mean?" Lincoln gave his partner his full attention.

"You know what I mean. Did you see the way she was looking at you? And not to mention the trance she put you in." Mike laughed.

"I ain't tripping off no woman right now. She just lost her husband, she ain't thinking about me." He thought back to their conversation earlier. He didn't think he would ever be able to bring her into his world. With his dead mother hanging around, Zachariah, and not to mention the vow he had made to God. She would never understand his life.

"I guess." Mike shook his head. He had been around Lincoln for years now and had never seen him with a woman. He had never even heard him mention a woman. "What time will you be back to get me?" Lincoln looked around and hadn't even noticed that Mike had made it all the way to his home. He was so zoned out thinking about Gabrielle he lost track of time.

"In about an hour or so."

"A'ight." Mike got out of the car and Lincoln walked around to the driver's side. Once inside, he tried his best not speed off, he wanted to get back to the strip so badly he was ready to put on the sirens. When he pulled up on the strip, all the hookers spread out like cockroaches, but he kept his eyes locked on the one he had come for. The he/she tried to slip down a pathway on the side of a vacant building but Lincoln was on him. He parked his car right at the opening of the driveway, jumped out of his car, and gave pursuit with his stun gun in hand. He wasn't taking any chances that the big guy might be too strong for him.

"Freeze!" Lincoln yelled just as the hooker tried to jump over a fence. When he saw that he wasn't going to stop, he took aim and shot the wires at his ass just as he was about to flip over the fence. His body froze, fell to the ground, and twitched as the electrical currents shot through his body. Lincoln held on to the trigger as he walked up to him. He watched as his body jerked and convulsed all over the ground. With his finger still on the trigger, he made sure the hooker was out, and there would be no resistance. He knew the he/she was too heavy for him to carry, so he dragged him back down the pathway by the shirt he was wearing. It took only a minute to get him in to the car. Lincoln put all his muscles to use to get him into the backseat.

Once he got the prostitute secured, he jumped in the driver's seat and sped off. His pulse began to quicken at all the possibilities of what Zachariah would do to the he/she. This would most definitely prove to be very interesting.

He drove like a crazed maniac trying to get back to his home as quickly as possible. He couldn't get out of his seat fast enough.

"So put to death the sinful, earthly things," he heard a whisper say.

"Stop it, Mother, not now!" he gritted as he pulled the hooker out of the backseat. He hated the way she came and went as she pleased, driving him even crazier than he already was.

"I am your mother and you will not speak to me that way!" she yelled in his ear. "Have you and the ingrate Zachariah been consorting on how to hurt me even more?"

"I'm sorry, Mother, just let me do this." Even in death, she controlled his life.

"It's ok son."

Lincoln couldn't help but to think about the fact that in death she knew who he was, but when she was alive, ninety percent of the time she had no clue as to who he was. Why is she still here? he asked himself. At first, it was comforting to have her around. Even though he had Jill there was nothing like the soothing voice of your biological mother. Now, he just wanted her to go away, to die again. He was so enraged that he nixed his whole plan for the hooker and did something he hadn't done in years. Right there in his backyard he grabbed an ax and swung it at the prostitute's neck chopping his head off with one swift strike of the ax. He imagined it was his mother. He swung that ax until the he/she was in tiny pieces spread out in his backyard. His chest heaved in and out like he had just run a marathon. Thoughts of the way his mother tortured him as a child ran rapidly in his head with each swing of the ax. With every swing, he was fighting her back; he was putting an end to her torture. In less than thirty seconds, his mother had ruined a routine that he and Zachariah had been doing for years. He had made a vow never to kill again, but Dorothy had gotten under his skin and made him go against his word.

"Good job son."

"Go away!" he cried at the realization of what he had done and the fact that she would never leave him. He dropped to his knees in a fit of tears.

"You want to pray my child?"

"No I want you to go away, why are still here, why won't you leave me alone?" Even as a child he never questioned God about what was happening to him, but now, he felt like he needed answers. Was he chosen? Why wouldn't his mother leave? He had so many "whys" with no answers coming and that alone was driving his insanity to the next level.

"I am here to make sure you stay on track, I will always be with you son."

He jumped up and ran into the shed to find Julia dead. From the looks of things, she had tried to squeeze her way out of the harness but it had gotten caught around her neck. From what he could see, Zachariah had really punished her from the grotesque sight before him. Her arms were still handcuffed to the base of the contraption so it looked like her shoulders were dislocated the way her body sank down the middle of the harness. The little critters of the night had come to feast upon her shredded flesh. The smell of rotting flesh and her final bowl movement assaulted his senses and brought up the food he had eaten earlier that night. Lincoln felt sorry for the way she had died, that's not what he wanted for her. He planned to end her quickly but had gotten sidetracked. He had a big mess to clean before he had to go back to pick up Mike.

Lincoln had to collect himself before he touched Julia. It seemed like she had every insect God ever made on her. One of his biggest fears was getting an insect inside of his ears or nose. The thought of it happening made his skin crawl.

He gathered all the pieces of the hooker he had chopped, unshackled Julia, and pushed her body off the harness with his foot careful not to get anything on him.

Then he dragged her to the pile where he had piled all of the other prostitute's body parts. While piling the wood and leaves on top of them, he cried. He felt what little sanity he had left was quickly making itself scarce. He just prayed that he got it together before he lost all control of his life.

The bodies were too bloody to put back in the car and his level of energy was too low to try to carry them down to the lake, so he opted to burn them. The irony of this was he was sure they were going to burn in hell for all eternity for their sins anyway. He felt like he was just preparing their souls for what was to come.

The smell of burning fleshing attacked his air intake; he needed to get away. He went in to take a shower. After showering, he went back out to make sure everything was in ashes. Lincoln loved living out in the woods with no neighbors for miles. He knew that was why his mother had gotten away with everything she had done to him; no one could hear him crying.

Once he was sure everything was ok, he left to go get Mike so they could finish their shift.

8
MAKE YOU LUV ME

Gabrielle lay in her hotel room thinking about Lincoln. She wondered what he was doing at that moment. Was she invading his every personal thought, as he was doing to her? She closed her eyes to see him in the private hiding spot she had stored his image in. She could see the scars on his face and even the scar going across his neck that he tried to hide. However, she didn't care about any of that. She felt like they were kindred spirits. They could share stories about the war wounds that they both had. She had plenty of stories to tell if he wanted to listen and she would let him tell her his whole life story if he wanted. She wanted to be near him, he made her feel safe. She was drawn to him like a moth to a flame. She smiled at the thought of seeing him again.

Throwing caution to the wind, she got up and got

dressed to go meet him when his shift ended. She looked at the clock and could see she had about an hour before he was to get off, figuring the regular nightshift hours would end between seven and seven thirty .

Gabrielle wanted to look good for him, he had only seen her looking a mess, and she wanted him to know she cleaned up well. She picked out a yellow maxi dress that came to her ankles and showed her curves in a tasteful way. Her multicolored wedges added the height that she needed. She didn't want to over dress. That might have scared him off, but she want to be noticed. With a hint of eye make-up and lip-gloss, she was ready to steal his heart.

It was warm and the sun was radiating its beautiful rays down on Gabrielle. She looked to the sky for some sort of guidance because she had absolutely no idea as to what she was doing. It was as if something was guiding her steps. If the forces of nature were guiding her to Lincoln, she would definitely follow them, no matter the path they took.

There was a feeling flowing through Gabrielle's body and she wasn't sure what it was just yet, but she welcomed it. She had decided on a whim to stop and get them some breakfast so they could eat in the park. She had already made up her mind that he would not turn her down.

As she pulled up to the police station, Lincoln and Mike were standing outside talking to a couple of other policemen. She swallowed the lump that had formed in her throat. All the confidence she had a few seconds prier flew out the window once she saw him standing there smiling with his friends. Instantly, she began to perspire all over. At that moment, she thanked God she had put some powder in the inside of her thighs. Butterflies were throwing a party inside of her stomach as she opened her door and headed towards him.

She tried not to feel self-conscious but her late husband Greg had always made it a point to let her know she was ugly and no one would ever want her. She was sweating so badly she felt the sweat dripping down the back of her legs. Her nerves had gotten the best of her so she turned to make a quick getaway before she was spotted.

"Gabrielle!" Lincoln called out after Mike had brought her presence to his attention. When she turned around to look at him, Lincoln couldn't believe how beautiful she was. "Damn," he whispered."

"Damn right, she is beautiful, alright Mr. Lincoln," the other police officers cheered him on. He smiled shyly. The closer she got, the more stunning she appeared to be.

"Hi," she said once she got in front of him. She smiled a smile so bright that it rivaled the brilliance of the sun. He watched as she strutted up to him as if she was walking a Victoria's Secret runway.

"How are you doing, what brings you here?" Lincoln asked while he admired her as her hair and dress blew in the wind. Her eyes had a sparkle in them that wasn't there before. The sun hit her irises at the perfect angle giving off the effect that they were about six different shades of brown.

"Hm," Mike cleared his throat while the other officers left Lincoln and Gabrielle to talk, but Mike wasn't budging until he met the lady that had his partner going to such lengths to protect her.

"Oh, this is my partner Mike and Mike this is Gabrielle." Lincoln laughed because he knew Mike wasn't going anywhere until he got to meet her.

"Hi, Mike, nice to meet you." She smiled his way then gave Lincoln her full attention again. "I came to see if we could go eat some breakfast." She held up the bags she had in her hands.

"Oh…um…sure." He hadn't even noticed the bags in her hands; he was too busy looking into her eyes. He looked back at Mike and he was just standing there with a stupid grin on his face. He knew Mike would be absolutely no help in getting out of this. So reluctantly, he went on what he considered his first date ever.

"So tell me a little about you Lincoln," Gabrielle said as they sat the in the park and ate the spread that she had put together. Orange juice, grapefruit, strawberries, and croissants were on the menu for them. She stared at him as he placed the cup of orange juice up to his mouth and wondered what it would be like to kiss him. To her he was the most beautiful man she had ever seen. She saw the beauty in his pain and it made her want to love him even more. She was determined to get into his head and see what was going on in there.

"There is really nothing to tell, you know I'm a police officer. I'm twenty five, no kids, and never been married." He hated talking about himself. That's why he avoided meeting new people. His life was one long horror movie and the less people he involved the better. What was he supposed to tell her? That his mother tried to kill him when he was child, his mind split in two, Zachariah was born, and that he was the will of the Lord and he punished sinners? He knew she would run for the hills and never look back. "How about you?"

"Really?" She looked at him suspiciously because obviously, from all the scars, there was more to his story, but she wouldn't push him. "Ok I'm twenty eight, I was married." She paused to see his reaction; he showed no signs of emotion at the mention of her husband. "No children, I was a housewife and wasn't allowed to work." She hunched her shoulders. There really was nothing more to her at least not that she could see. Since her husband was killed, she was trying to learn herself again and get to know what she liked and didn't like.

"Have the police said anything to you about your husband being killed? You know we always suspect the spouse first?" He laughed.

"Yes the morning it happened they called and woke me up out of my sleep. When I got there, my house was burned down to the ground. Nothing but ash, they asked me where I had been and I told them. We went downtown, they questioned me some more until my alibi checked out, and they let me go. But I have a feeling they will be back because I heard one of the firemen say that there was an accelerant used in the fire. So I guess they have to do more investigating." She shrugged her shoulders as she bit into one the strawberries. He watched as a little bit of juice escaped the side of her mouth. He fought the urge to lick it off.

"Oh ok, well at least they let you go." He knew he would do whatever he needed to keep her from being blamed for the murder. Even if he had to frame someone else for the deed.

"I know right." She regarded him; he had a far off look in his eyes, like he was really thinking about something. She would give anything to know what he was thinking. He seemed like such a complicated man, but she wanted to learn everything about him, all his wants, and desires. She was willing to do anything for him.

"Ok well I have to be going; I worked a long shift last night." He needed to get away from Gabrielle. The more he stayed around her the more he wanted her, but he knew they could never be a couple. Once again, he wanted to ask God why he had been cursed to live such a life. Why couldn't he be happy? However, he never questioned his mission in life.

"So soon, I thought we would sit and talk for a bit." She looked disappointed. "Can I see you again?" She looked at him and could tell he was fighting within himself about something.

"I don't think that would be a good idea." He

shook his head as he looked up into the sun. He couldn't even look at her because he knew he would take his words back, but that would only cause her more problems. He was a monster in gentlemen's clothing. He felt like he was unlovable and undeserving of love. With the double life he led, he knew he would eventually burn in hell. There was no way God would let him into heaven with everything that Zachariah had done, even if it was in his name.

"But why? I don't understand." Her feelings were hurt and she didn't hide it. At that moment, she felt like the lowest form of scum on the earth. Why she couldn't get a man to love her was beyond her comprehension. What had she done in her past lives to deserve what she was going through? She just wanted to be happy and she felt that she and Lincoln could be happy together.

"You don't want to be with me. You think I did something for you that I didn't do. I can't make you happy. I'm no good for you." He stood up and began to walk away.

"Lincoln wait!" she called to him as she walked up to him. When he turned around, she was standing in his face. Lincoln felt a heat in his groin area being so close to her. "How do you know you can't make me happy? I'm standing here willing to let you try." She walked in closer. "I want to learn everything there is to know about you. I want to be the reason you smile in the morning and dream sweet dreams at night."

She didn't even know the man standing in front

of her but she knew she wanted him. She reached out and touched his face as she looked up into his unsure eyes. She rubbed the scars on his face. "You don't have to do anything, just let me show you how to love me." She pulled his face down to hers and planted a long wet kiss on his lips. He didn't react at first. It took a few seconds before he wrapped his arms around her waist and pulled her in to embrace her softness. Their tongues danced in each other's mouths sending shockwaves through their bodies.

Lincoln had never felt anything like the feeling that was coursing through his body. Her body seemed to melt on to him, she fit perfectly in his arms, and if he could, he would keep her there forever. The feeling was getting too good. He felt his manhood rising for the occasion, so he pushed back from her and stepped back.

"I can't do this right now, I'm sorry." He turned and jogged away. He fought the urge to turn around and go back to her. He wanted to look at her one more time, but that would only make leaving worse. He knew it would be best for her if he just left. He could only imagine the pain she was feeling at that moment because it was breaking his heart to walk away from her. He just hoped she would stay away.

Gabrielle stood there stunned to silence. She couldn't believe he just walked away from her. She knew he felt the sparks when their lips touched. The energy that passed between them was earth shattering. She would not be discouraged from her mission. He would be hers. She needed him and she could tell he needed her, he just didn't know it yet. She had no problem with making him love her.

9
WEAKNESS OF THE FLESH

Lincoln could still feel the warmth of Gabrielle's lips on his as he lay in bed thinking about her. He couldn't shake her from his thoughts. She had done what she set out to do; she had invaded his every thought. She had put a permanent smile on his heart with one kiss.

He imagined his hands were her lips as he greased them up and began to stroke himself. With every stroke of his hand, his dick got harder. He moaned as he envisioned her head going up and down slowly making sure she got the whole thing sloppy wet. He stroked himself to the point of no return. He picked up his pace as he fucked her face hard taking him to a euphoric high as he shot his cum down the back of her throat. His eyes and teeth were clenched shut until the moment subsided.

When Lincoln opened his eyes, his mother was

standing there with a scowl on her face. "You nasty sinner, I should have cut it off when I had the chance!" Lincoln jumped out of the bed with his dick dripping sperm all over the floor. He covered himself up with his hands as best he could. His heart beat at a rapid speed, giving him the feeling of a heart attack. He whipped his head back and forth to see where she had gone. Had she been there the whole time watching him? Just as quickly as she had appeared, she had disappeared.

Lincoln knew he would have to get a grip on things if he ever wanted a chance to be with Gabrielle or even a chance at a normal life. He walked into the bathroom to get into the shower. As he stood under the steamy shower thoughts of what his mother had said replayed. I should have cut it off when I had the chance. He shook his head trying to get the memory out of his head but he had already begun going down memory lane.

"What are doing sinner?" His mother walked into his bedroom catching him playing with himself.

"Huh? Nothing Mother I had an itch." Lincoln pulled his covers up to his chin. He was embarrassed that his mother had caught him playing with his private parts. At the tender age of eight, he was fascinated with everything about his penis. It was abnormally large for his age, but he didn't know that because his mother never talked to him about his body parts growing. However, he admired his penis, often wondering what he was supposed to with it. Why was it shaped the way it was and how much bigger would it get? Those were all questions that he thought about on a daily basis. All he knew was he liked the way it felt when he rubbed it, he would watch it and count to see how long it took him to get hard.

"You nasty little liar, I'm going to show you what the Lord does to people who thinks it's ok to masturbate." She went into her room to grab a razor and came back in time to see Lincoln standing in the middle his room in a pair of dirty white briefs trying to find a place to hide.

"Mother, please, I won't do it anymore," he pleaded as he watched her walk towards him with the razor in her hand. The wild look in her eyes let him know she was dead serious. "Mother what are you going to do with that?" He didn't want her to cut his thing off. He began to cry hysterically at the thought of being cut down there.

"Come here sinner, you won't need it anyway, no one will ever want you," she sneered as she yanked him by the arm towards her. She got down on her knees in front of him and pulled his little briefs down. His penis jumped out into her face. She took hold of it and looked at him. He shook as if he had a high fever.

"Please Mother I won't do it anymore. I promise. I'll pray for forgiveness," he cried as she held his penis in her hand.

"The Lord doesn't hear the pleas of sinners. Look at you getting aroused because I'm touching it." She frowned. "That's why we have to get rid of it. The flesh is weak when temptation is too strong."

She took the razor and sliced him across the groin area.

"Ahhhhh!" he screamed and pushed at his mother's head to trying to get her away from him, but she held on tightly, she was squeezing his penis so hard he thought she would break it. "Mother stop! Please don't do that anymore!" he begged as he watched blood drip down his legs onto the floor.

"We must get rid of this, sinner." This time she sliced down his penis and he fainted. When he woke up he was covered in blood and his penis had cuts all over it. Dorothy was gone into another room. He was in a lot of pain but he was happy she hadn't cut it off. He was sore for weeks and the healing process was even harder than when she had cut him. She had cut him so badly; he was barely able to hold his blooming manhood while he peed, and when the cuts began to heal, the scabs would rub against his underwear and make the cuts feel fresh all over again.

The water turning cold brought Lincoln out his thoughts. He turned the water off and got out of the shower. He looked down at his dick and looked at all the scars his mother had left on him. He wondered what stopped her from cutting it off when she was so close to it. He sat down on the edge of his bed and thought about Gabrielle. He had to have her no matter the consequences. The feeling was too strong to avoid anymore.

Lincoln went to his dresser to find the pills he had to take when he wanted his mother to go away. When he was given the pills as a child to help with his nightmares and delusions, he didn't want to take them. He liked having his mother visit with him and pray with him. However, as he grew older, his mother's visits became too much for him some times so he started taking them when he wanted his thoughts to stay private and the nightmares to stop. He popped one, threw on some gray sweat pants, a tank top, and a pair of Air Max. He looked in the mirror at his attire and wondered if he was doing the right thing. The only people who ever saw his scars were Jill and Mike.

"She said she wanted to know everything," he said to himself as he inhaled deeply, blew an exaggerated breath out, and headed out the door.

*****

Gabrielle sat in the windowpane with her legs pulled up to her chest, looking down on the streets of St. Louis thinking about Lincoln. When she had gotten back from their breakfast date she got undressed and had been sitting in the window for hours just thinking. It was peaceful up there on the eleventh floor. She watched as a plane flew over the building and wondered where it was going and wished she were on it, so it could take her away from the pain that overwhelmed her every day. It didn't matter where it was going; she just needed to get away.

Gabrielle wanted to try to forget about Lincoln but his image was sketched in her mind's eye and she couldn't seem to shake her thoughts of him.

Ever since the first time she saw him in the police station, she felt something magnetic pulling her to him. She reasoned that out of all the police officers in the station, how had she found him? Why was he the one to be there to hear her plea? She didn't understand what was going on. All she knew was that she wanted to be near him. She looked around her hotel room it was lonely there and it made her think of her late husband. Regret was never a factor; the only thing she regretted was the fact that she wasn't there to see him take his last breath.

In the beginning of their marriage, everything was perfect. As usual, she was young and he spoiled her. He was older and gave her that security she had never had in her father. However, somewhere along the line, he became a monster and love turned to hate. He began beating her on a daily basis just because the sky was blue. He wasn't a drunk or anything in the beginning so she didn't know where it all came from. She thought about the babies she had lost and rubbed her stomach. At first, she didn't understand why she kept losing them, but eventually, she reasoned that God knew she couldn't bring a baby into the world she was living in. She thought about her family and wondered if they would accept her back into their fold. Greg had stopped all communication with them. Now that he was gone, she was scared at the thought of them rejecting her.

Thoughts of Greg quickly went away though, she would rather be lonely than miserable. She wanted to thank Lincoln for what he had done for her but he wouldn't even admit to the good deed. Even though he denied it, she knew the truth; she could feel it in her heart that he had helped her. All she wanted was to help him; she could tell he needed someone to help him. His eyes looked so sad, even when he smiled at her, she could see a sadness in them. She didn't know who had hurt him but if she could she would take away his pain, she would gladly bear his agony with him.

She heard a knock at her door; she got up and put on a robe because she was naked as the day she was born. Without looking out the peephole, she pulled the door open, and there stood Lincoln. She stood stunned at the sight before her. She looked his body over and could see all the scars that covered his body. His uniform hid them well.

Lincoln stood there letting her eyes roam all over his body. Her eyes scanned every part of his exposed skin. He wanted her to see what he was, a monster, but the way she was looking at him didn't say she saw a monster, he saw love and empathy in her eyes. She stepped closer to him and reached out to rub the scar going across his neck. He didn't flinch; he would let her take it all in. No words were spoken but the silence spoke volumes. He watched her watch him as she stepped back, untied her robe, and let it fall to the floor. Lincoln took a step closer to her, picked her up, and she wrapped her legs around his waist as he kicked the door shut and carried her to the bed.

As he lay her down on the bed, he sat up and pulled his wife beater over his head. Once again, she stared in wonderment at the mutilations that adorned his body. She rubbed her hand all over his chest as she used her legs to pull him back down to her. She wanted to drink his essence, to become one with him. She would submit to his every desire if only he'd give her the chance. He pushed his tongue into her mouth and she hungrily sucked it into her mouth. Their tongues did a slow dance as their hands explored each other's bodies. He wrapped his arms around her and rolled over so she was on top of him. His hands explored her body and she moaned as his hands massaged her ass cheeks. He lifted her up into the air and pulled her up until she was sitting on his face. The moment his tongue touched her hot box she felt a shock shoot through her body. She moaned as her body bucked every time his tongue slipped across her clit.

Lincoln's tongue was making her dizzy with desire. She had never in her life felt anything like what Lincoln was doing to her. She felt an orgasm coming on that started in her toes and crept slowly up her body, making her spine tingle. Then a tingly sensation took over her love tunnel as she let out a load scream that she was sure the whole building had heard.

"Shit...sssssss," she cursed and hissed as the feeling started to subside.

Lincoln never let up on her clit. He loved the way her essence tasted on his tongue. Her love juices flooded his mouth and he happily sucked and swallowed every ounce. He had never wanted to please a woman so badly in his life. He moved his tongue all around making sure he had caught every drop of her juices. He held her up because her body had gone limp but he wasn't finished yet. He finally lay her down and spread her legs as far as they would go and stuck his face right back down in her pussy making her scream out.

Gabrielle pushed at his head to make him stop but he was like an animal getting his first meal of the day. He wasn't letting her clit go; he held it in his mouth sucking on it hard bringing on another orgasm that Gabrielle didn't think she would be ready for. She couldn't run; he had her pinned down, so she lay there and let him take her on an exhilarating high as shock waves of ecstasy rippled through her body. She looked down at Lincoln and could see he was watching her as he pleasured her. He had this intense look in his eyes that let her know he was determined in what he was doing. She closed her eyes and bit her bottom lip as she pulled at the sheets on the bed. Her body was feeling things she didn't even know was possible.

When her orgasm subsided, he came back up and softly kissed her on the forehead and turned her so he was laying behind her. He wrapped his arms around her, pulled her into his embrace, and just held her. Gabrielle was shocked that he hadn't tried to have sex with her. She wanted him to make love to her but she wouldn't push the subject. She was glad he lay behind her so he couldn't see the disappointment sketched across her face. She was just happy he was there at that point, so she would take whatever she could get. Lincoln had decided that he was going to give himself to her slowly. Even though he could see she honestly didn't care about any of his scars, he knew there was no getting around explaining the scars on his penis. It wasn't the time for all that. He just wanted to please her and pleasing her pleased him so everyone was content for the moment.

Gabrielle melted into his arms and drifted off to sleep. Lincoln did the same, the fatigue from not having slept since before his shift took over his body.

A few hours later, Gabrielle woke up, saw that she was still in Lincoln's arms, and smiled. She hadn't been dreaming; he really did come over and rock her world. They hadn't had sex but he had her floating through the clouds. His mouth made love to her soul as his hands took hold of her heart. She turned so she was facing him. There was a slight smile on his face and she wondered what he was dreaming about.

Lincoln had been dreaming of Gabrielle and how good she tasted on his tongue. The feeling of her lying in his arms, her skin felt like Egyptian silk under his touch. Every spot on her body he touched he felt a warmth there; he didn't know if it was because his body temperature had risen to an inferno or if she was as hot as he was. Either way, he loved the way she felt up against his body.

"When you follow the desires of your sinful nature, the results are very clear," Lincoln's mother began as she invaded his dream, but he cut her off by wrapping his hands around neck. He was tired of her and wanted her to just go away.

"Leave me alone," he gritted as he tried to squeeze all her ghostly life out of her.

"Ha ha you can't get rid of me," she laughed at his attempt at killing her again. She looked into his eyes defiantly taunting him.

"Lin...coln...stop...stop!" Gabrielle cried as she scratched at his hands. He had this crazy far off look in his eyes as if he wasn't even looking at her, but his eyes were staring into hers. It was as if he was seeing someone else.

"Leave me alone, I just want to be happy." Lincoln had completely zoned out. He applied more pressure trying to crush his mother's esophagus. "Just die! Die!"

"Lincoln!" Gabrielle screamed as she felt her body getting weak. "It's me! Wake up!" She reached up and dug her nails in his face. The pain snapped Lincoln out of his dream world and when saw a scared Gabrielle under him with his hands wrapped around her throat he wanted to curl up in a ball and die.

"Oh my God I'm so sorry!" He jumped out of the bed.

"It's ok you were having a nightmare," she reasoned as she rubbed her neck. She tried to make it seem like it wasn't a big deal but she knew it was. He was way more messed up than she thought.

"No it's not ok; this is why we can't be together. I'm no good for you. I'm damaged," he confessed.

"My life has been fucked up since birth and I would never want to bring you into my world."

"Let me help you." She stood up and began to walk towards him. He put his hand up.

"People have been trying to help me out my whole life and it never works out so don't even bother with the let me help you speech. I don't need your fucking help!" he yelled.

"But Lincoln…"

"Don't come closer; I have to go." He grabbed his shirt and tried to walk out of the door.

"You are not going to keep running from me." Gabrielle blocked his way. She refused to let him just leave again. They were going to talk this out.

"Move Gabrielle," he pleaded. He just wanted to leave, his mother would forever be a fixture in his life, and he knew no one would ever understand that. She tortured him in life and now in death. The pills only helped half the time now.

"No, talk to me dammit!" she demanded.

"Talk to you about what?" he yelled making her jump back. "About how my mother did this to me?" he pointed to the scar around his neck. "About how she beat and starved me damn near every day of my life. How every scar on my body was cause by my mother? My mother did this shit to me! My damn mother!" He banged his fist up against his chest. He didn't know why he kept repeating the words, "My mother." Maybe it was because he had never said those words out loud before.

Gabrielle stood dumbfounded. She had absolutely nothing to say. Never had she imagined his mother was the one who did that to him.

"I didn't think so." He picked her up, moved her out of the way, and walked out of the door. His heart wanted him to go back; his body missed her the moment he walked out of the door. He didn't mean to explode on her the way he did but she kept pushing. At least now, she knew a little more about him, maybe not, what she had in mind, but info was info wasn't it?

10
AND SO A BEAST WAS BORN

And I stood upon the sand of the sea, and
saw a beast rise up out of the sea, having
seven heads and ten horns, and upon his
horns ten crowns, and upon his heads the
name of blasphemy.

"What is your name sinner?" Lincoln asked as
he towered over his latest victim. After everything
that happened with Gabrielle, he needed a release.
Zachariah would not be enjoying this one, so he
went looking for a sinner after he did his regular
routine of dropping Mike off with his wife for a
while. He had spotted the young lady giving head in
an alley and thought he had the perfect thing for
such a filthy mouth.

"Daija," she cried. She looked around at the shed she was in. It looked like a medieval torture chamber and it reeked of death. She could see dingy bloodstains on the walls that someone must have missed. Tools, chains, and hooks covered the walls giving off a dungeon feeling. She prayed whatever he was about to do to her would be quick. It was just her luck that on her first night out on the strip she would get picked up by a psychopath. She had lost her job and was about to be evicted. Her friend who worked the strip told her to come down for the night and guaranteed her at least her rent money would be made. She reasoned it would only be one night.

She was strapped into the harness but Lincoln wouldn't make the same mistake twice. She would die as soon as he finished his business with her. He had set her up the same way he had Julia.

"Do you know why I have brought you're here, sinner?" he questioned as he began to take his clothes off.

"No sir." She watched every move he made. Once he had gotten his shirt off, she gasped. "Wh...why am I here?" she stuttered as she tore her eyes away from his scar filled torso. His body looked like it had he gone through a meat shredder and she prayed he wasn't going to do that to her. She turned her back towards him and her jaw hit the floor once he dropped his pants. That can't be real, she thought.

"You have been judged and the Lord has sent me to do his will." He walked to the back of her.

"Please sir, I was just trying to pay my rent. I don't do that kind of stuff on a regular," she tried to plead her case. "Please I swear I won't do it anymore." She twisted her neck trying to see what he was doing behind her.

Lincoln kneeled down behind her and closed his eyes as he envisioned Gabrielle was in front of him. He rubbed his hands up her body and massaged her breast as he kissed and licked all her back.

"Hmmmmm," Daija moaned forgetting her current situation for a minute.

"Don't make a sound," he gritted as he yanked her head back by her hair. Her voice had thrown him off a little, so he dug deep into his memory bank and thought about how Gabrielle sounded when she moaned for him earlier. Her moans were whispering sweet nothings in his ear. He went back to doing what he was doing before she had interrupted him.

Lincoln let out a moan, he was relishing in the taste of her body as licked down her back. There was a faint scent of pineapples on her skin. He nibbled on her ass cheeks as he greased himself up. That was the one thing that was fucking up his fantasy. He knew he wouldn't need any grease with Gabrielle; he would have her pussy creaming and overflowing. He gripped Daija's waist as he guided himself into her. She was extra tight not like the loose pussies he had encountered over the years with prostitutes. No doubt in his mind, she wasn't lying about not being a professional woman of the night, but she still had to go.

Daija wanted to scream out but was too scared of what he might do to her. She was too scared to breathe let alone make any sounds. His unmeasurable phallus penetrating her felt like someone had placed a hot pole inside of her. He was stretching her walls to the point where she knew there should have been blood somewhere. She couldn't front though, his stroke was wonderful, and he knew exactly what he was doing with his pole. His thrusting felt so good it confused her. It felt like he was making love to her the way he gripped her hips and moaned with each stroke into her aching hot box.

Lincoln stroked her nice and slow like he would do to Gabrielle. He hadn't even put all of himself into her; he wanted her to get used to his size. All women's love tunnels were tight to Lincoln and normally he would give it all to them at once, but not this time, he wanted to be gentle with Gabrielle. Slowly, he inched his way deeper into Daija's hot box. She didn't know how he was feeling but for her the sex was feeling wonderful. She hadn't been made love to like that in all her life. The pain his dick had been bringing was quickly turning to pleasure. She knew women who would kill just to hold a dick of his magnitude. She didn't know who he was imaging she was, but she knew when he actually got a hold of her he was going to rock her world.

Lincoln bit his bottom lip to keep his moaning in check. Her walls were welcoming all of him to go deep into her love tunnel. Daija's juices had started flowing freely down his shaft. He could see a coat of white foam on his penis and he looked at it curiously, having never seen it before. He dug his nails into her shoulders as pulled her back hard on to his dick.

"Ooh shit Gabrielle this pussy so tight I love it," Lincoln grunted. Daija wanted to scream out but thought better of it. She felt like he had just pushed all her insides up into her chest cavity.

Lincoln was lost in his thoughts as he hit her with the death stroke. He wanted Gabrielle in the worst way, but after earlier; he knew their future would be turbulent and not end well. He felt his balls tighten up as a tingly sensation settled in the bottom of his sack. He pushed her ass cheeks apart and pushed himself in until he could go no further.

"Ssssss," he hissed as he pumped harder into her love box trying to get the orgasm to surface. Once he felt himself releasing his cum into her, his teeth clenched shut as every muscle in his body flexed and tightened. He shivered as her pussy constricted around his pole to milk the last of his nut out. After catching his breath, he removed himself from within her and stood up with his dick covered in her juices and his cum. He walked around to front her and squatted down so they were face to face. She looked up into his eyes and could see this was where she would die. His look said he didn't want to do it but he had to. Her body instantly went numb and tears flooded out of her eyes. She couldn't understand how every women on that strip had avoided this lunatic and on her first night out she was about to die.

"Please Lord Jesus I'm sorry for my sins, please accept my apologies, and welcome me into heaven," Daija prayed she made it to heaven.

"I truly am sorry. You just happened to be in the place at the wrong time," Lincoln paused for a minute but he couldn't leave her alive, so he reached up and grabbed her neck. In one swift motion, he twisted her neck breaking it instantly giving her a quick and painless death. It was her lucky day though, this was for him so the wrath of God would not be felt today, or at least she wouldn't be the one to feel it.

Lincoln took her body down to lake in the woods that was home to a few alligators and tossed her body in. He knew her remains would be gone in less than an hour. He had found that spot when he was younger. On one of his mother Dorothy's good days, she let him out to play and an alligator he didn't see sneaking up on him had almost eaten him. His mother didn't let him out too often but when she did, he would hunt small animals and take them to the lake to watch the gators eat.

After he cleaned himself up, he was on his way back to Mike. He looked down at the phone sitting on the seat and wanted to call Gabrielle, but he called someone else instead.

After a few rings, he heard a voice on the line.

"Hey baby!" Jill his adopted mother sang into the phone.

"Hey Momma."

"Lincoln is everything ok?" Jill looked at the clock and saw that it was three in the morning.

"Yes ma'am, you know I work the night shift and forget the rest of the world is asleep." He laughed.

"Oh it's ok, shoot I'm up now. What's going on baby?" She could sense something was going on with him.

"Nothing why you say that? I just wanted to talk to my momma."

"Yeah ok, spit it out boy, you got me a grandbaby on the way yet? You know I ain't getting no younger." She so desperately wanted him to meet someone and settle down. However, she had never seen him with a girl or heard him speak of a girl.

"No Ma! Nothing is cooking in nobody's oven but you will be happy to know that I have met someone," he admitted.

"Who, is she cute, what does she do, do she got any kids, she ain't no ghetto chick is she?" she rambled off question after question she was so excited.

"Her name is Gabrielle, that's all you get for now. I'm still trying to figure this whole thing out."

"She's not playing with your emotions is she? You know I will get her together," she threatened.

"No, calm down woman," he laughed. She could

always make him feel better. No matter what he had going on, he could call Jill, and she would put a smile on his heart.

"I'm just saying don't nobody be messing with my baby."

"Naw she cool, I'm just trying to figure out what I'm doing. You know all this is new to me," he confessed.

"Well baby just let it flow don't force it. And if it's meant to be it will all come together perfectly."

"Ok Momma I got to go, I'm picking up Mike," he said as Mike sat down in the passenger seat.

"Ok tell my lil' tendaroni I said hi and I want y'all to come to dinner soon."

"Really?" He shook his head. "Alright Momma, I'll tell him." He laughed at her trying to sound hip. "I love you Ma."

"Love you too baby"

"Hey Momma Jill!" Mike yelled in the background.

"She said hi fool," Lincoln said as he hung up the phone.

"You a hater, you know she gon' be my mistress one day. You gon' be calling me Poppa Mike," he bragged, he always thought Jill was flirting with him.

"Whatever! You better leave my damn momma alone." He laughed because ever since he had introduced them Mike had had a crush on Jill. She was a beautiful woman tall in stature with a caramel complexion. She aged gracefully and at the age of fifty, she didn't look a day over thirty.

"Aye what you be doing when you drop me off at night?" Mike blurted the question out catching Lincoln off guard. He had always wondered what Lincoln did. Lincoln never talked about his ventures at night. Mike figured he didn't just go sit at a restaurant for all that time.

"Huh?" Lincoln gave him a confused look.

"I mean what do you be doing, do you go and sit somewhere? Do you go pick up hookers?" He laughed at the last statement because he figured Lincoln wouldn't even know what to do with a hooker.

No one knew that Lincoln had learned all his skills from a hooker years ago. At the age of 18, he was still insecure about his scars. Because of them, he would never approach a girl too afraid of rejection, so he enlisted the help of a hooker named Monique he had known from around his neighborhood. She was an older lady with hard looking facial features, but she wasn't rough on the eyes though. He could tell the years had been turbulent on her, but who was he to judge her.

No matter how Monique's eyes looked, she kept her body in A1 condition; she believed her body would be her ticket out of the street life. Her D cup breasts still sat up at attention and her ass sat perfectly upon her back, with sprinter's legs, she held her own against the younger girls she ran with in the streets. She had taught him everything about pleasing a woman. She gave him a beginner's course on women's pleasure spots 101.

Lincoln had grown attached to her and found himself having feelings for her. He had bought all her nights for almost two months. After that, she would come for free. Lincoln wanted to believe that he could change her ways. What she did for a living no more bothered him than all the scars on his body bothered her. She understood him and treated him like a man. However, Dorothy did not approve of their little trysts, so she came to him and demanded that he punish her for her sins. That was the first time he killed and the last time he cried.

*****

"The Lord has spoken, Lincoln, she must go!" Dorothy demanded.

"No Mother I like her, she's the only person that is nice to me," he pleaded.

"Oh she nice 'cause she fornicates with you. That doesn't make her nice that makes her a whore. And do you think your little peewee is the only one she's sucking on?" she laughed at him for being so naive.

"Stop it Mother she's a nice lady. She talks to me and treats me like a man. I don't want to do it."

He was in love with a hooker and he knew his mother would never approve. To be a hooker was the oldest profession and the oldest sin in her eyes.

"Prostitutes been tricking men since the days of Judah!"

"I know Mother," Lincoln said hoping to avoid one of her lectures on the Bible.

"Oh you don't know nothing. After sleeping with two of Judah's sons, she was sent away because her forbidden fruit was spoiled rotten and couldn't bear kids. She came back to prove a point and sold her rotten twat to Judah for a damn goat!" Lincoln chuckled at the revelation. "So son I don't blame you. She has you under a spell is all."

"I understand all that but I want to be with her."

"Oh so are you telling the Lord no?" she challenged.

"No ma'am," he relented.

"Good now when she gets here you know what to do and don't you stick you little dick in her either. Just get it over with you hear me?"

"Yes Mother." Lincoln wanted to cry. He never wanted to hurt Monique but when it came to his mother there was no winning against her. He had never taken a human life before; he didn't know what he was getting himself into.

Lincoln heard a knock at the hotel room door. It was the same hotel they met at whenever they got together. Lincoln would have loved to have her in his bed but he knew Dorothy would go berserk at the thought a hooker being in her home.

"Hey honey dip. What's…" Monique's sentence stopped once she got all the way in the room and saw him standing with a metal shower rod in his hands and tears running down his face.

"I don't want to do this, but I have to." He charged towards her. She pulled a blade from her bra and swung it at him.

"What's going on Lincoln? Why are you trying to hurt me?" she asked as they circled each other. Never did she think she would need her weapon for Lincoln. He was the only bright spot in her life. Before meeting him, she hated everything about herself.

"I swear I don't want to do this but she won't leave me alone." He shook his head. The pain he was feeling was almost unbearable.

"Then don't do it Lincoln. This isn't for you and me. I love you." She had totally fallen for Lincoln. The men she slept with while working made her feel like the lowest form of life, but Lincoln made her feel as if she were an actual human being and treated her like a lady even knowing what she did for a living. Yes, he was a lot younger than she was, but he was the man she dreamed of coming to save her from herself.

"Lies all lies Lincoln, all those people do is lie." Dorothy could tell Monique's words were starting to get to the Lincoln.

"The Lord has spoken and you have been judged." He lunged at her again. This time both of them connected with each other at the same time. She sliced his arm and he hit her in the temple with the pole. He took a moment to assess his cut, but it wasn't that bad.

"It's time, son, time for you take on your duties as the Lord's will," Dorothy pushed him.

"Just shut up for a minute!" he yelled. Lincoln looked at the woman he loved and felt a burning in his heart that was almost crippling.

Lincoln took a deep and loomed over Monique's body. His heart was breaking with every passing second. He was unaware that Monique would be his first victim; he would have never made such an agreement.

"So put to death the sinful," Lincoln raised his arm that held the pole and brought it down on Monique's face, "earthly things lurking within you." He swung the pole again grunting with each swing. He felt so much hate and anger coursing through his veins that he began to sweat profusely and shake violently. "Have nothing to do with sexual immorality, impurity, lust, and evil desires." More grunts escaped his mouth as he cried tears of anger. He was angry with God for making him kill the woman he loved and his mother for cheering him on as she prayed over his shoulder. "Don't be greedy, for a greedy person is an idolater." He swung the pole again and again turning Monique's head into a crimson mush. "Worshiping the things of the world." He dropped to his knees and cried over Monique's dead body. His heart had been shattered into a million pieces. And in one night, in a matter of minutes, a beast was born. "Because of these sins, the anger of God is coming.

"Aye man, I'm sitting here talking to you and you haven't heard a word I've said to you." Mike nudged Lincoln bringing back to the present time.

"Aw damn my bad you know I be zoning out sometimes." Lincoln still felt the pain of that night every time he thought about it. He could still smell stench that lingered in the hotel room, the way Monique's fragrance of choice filled the atmosphere when she walked in. He could never forget how she smelled. She wore the same perfume every day and it smelled like cotton candy to him.

"I'm sorry, what were you saying?" He gave Mike his undivided attention.

"I said what happened with Gabrielle?"

"Nothing really, we went to eat." Lincoln shrugged his shoulders. He wasn't ready to give any details, because he wasn't sure of what he was going to do just yet. His body yearned for her touch and his eyes had a craving to feast on her smile. However, his brain knew better.

"That's it?"

"Yeah, what you thought we were going to do, get naked and screw in the park?" Lincoln laughed.

"Hell you could have and that would have been better than the sorry shit you telling me right now," Mike laughed.

"Well there is nothing to tell. Sorry to ruin your moment."

11
HE LOVES ME NOT

It had been days since Gabrielle heard from Lincoln and she was going crazy out of her mind. He was definitely a hard one to figure out. She thought if she gave him some time he would come around. However, he hadn't called nor answered any of her phone calls. It was time for her to check out of her hotel room and she had absolutely nowhere to go, but she wouldn't change a thing, if she had to sleep in her car she would. She didn't have the insurance money yet, and she figured she wouldn't until they were finished investigating. It had been a week since Greg's death and she had no idea where his ashes were and didn't care to ask neither. Just knowing she didn't have to endure another moment with Greg was well worth it.

"Hi I'm in room 1102 what time do I have to

check out?" Gabrielle spoke into the phone.

"Um let me check Ms. Tymes. You're a little early ma'am; your room has been paid up for the month. Did you want to leave early?" the clerk asked.

"No I wasn't trying to leave; I must have forgotten I paid the bill already. When was the bill paid?" she asked shocked and happy. She had thought she was about to be out on her ass.

"Yesterday night."

"You wouldn't happen to know who paid it, would you?" She had a feeling who it was she just wanted to hear him say it aloud.

"No ma'am it was paid with cash."

"Ok, thank you." Gabrielle hung up and looked around her room at what little stuff she was able to pack up in a hurry the night she left her husband. She barely had anything because most of her belongings were burned in the fire. However, those things could be replaced, and her life couldn't. Once again, she thanked God for placing Lincoln in her life. Just a week ago, she was battered and bruised, crying her heart out, but Lincoln had freed her, and now she was at peace. She wanted to pick up the phone to call him but she was tired of the rejection, so she opted to take nap for the time being.

*****

"Gabrielle!" she heard Greg yell as he walked through the door. Gabrielle rolled her eyes because she could hear unnecessary anger in his voice. She got up and wobbled her seven months pregnant body into the living room where he was standing.

"Yes Greg, what is it?" she huffed as she looked at him and frowned. It felt like she was carrying a hundred pound baby in her stomach. Her ankles were swollen and she was exhausted, but she wouldn't trade the feeling of being pregnant for nothing in the world. She had been waiting for years to have her first-born child.

"Where is my dinner?" He waved his arms around wildly.

"You told me you ate already, when I called to see if you wanted anything." She knew it was about to be some shit because they had talked an hour before and he told her not worry about fixing dinner because he would be late, but now here he was asking for a meal.

"You don't do shit else around this muthafucka and I can't even get dinner?" He charged towards her, grabbed her by the back of her neck, and led her into the kitchen.

"Please calm down Greg I will get you something to eat."

"Shut the fuck up! You are the most useless piece of shit to ever fall out a pussy."

"You told me you wouldn't hit me this time while I was pregnant," she cried. She had been pregnant four times before this and this was the furthest she had ever gotten.

"Bitch how you gon' tell me what I can can't do

in my house? You don't pay no fucking bills around this bitch!" he roared, outraged at her blatant disrespect. He threw her into the refrigerator. "You better get yo' ass up and fix me something to eat," he demanded.

"Ok." Gabrielle looked up at him and saw the devil looking back her. Her tears seemed to be endless. Every day she cried for one reason or another. He promised he wouldn't hit her again while she was pregnant.

Gabrielle waited for him to leave the room before she moved out of the spot he pushed her in. When she heard the bedroom door slam, she dropped down to her knees and cried. She didn't know how much more she would be able to take. She was crying so hard that she didn't hear him when he walked back in to the kitchen.

"The fuck you crying for? I haven't even done nothing yet." He looked around and saw that she hadn't started cooking yet. "See this the shit I be talking about!" he yelled as he pulled her up off the floor and held her by the collar of her shirt.

"Please no, I'm starting, no please," she begged him.

"Bitch I'd be dead by the time you finished!" He smacked her across her face sending her flying over the kitchen table. She landed on her stomach and knew something was wrong instantly, but he didn't care.

"Please, wait, the baby!" she shrieked as she was trying to lift herself up off the floor. She felt a pain go across her back like she had been sliced. The pain wrapped around her torso taking her breath away. "I need help, please," she pleaded to deaf ears.

"You want to cry? I'm gon' give you something to cry for!" She looked up just in time to see him bringing his arm down with a belt in his hand.

"Please, no, wait, stop!" Gabrielle screamed as she sat straight up out of her nightmare sweating and panting like she had just run up a flight stares. Her eyes darted around the room and saw that she was alone and there was no Greg there to hurt her anymore. He was gone and she had to get used that.

Gabrielle rubbed her stomach at the thought of the child she had lost that day. She wanted kids but didn't even know if it was possible anymore with all the damage that had been done to her body. Greg used her as his personal toilet, punching bag, sex slave, whatever he wanted her to be on any particular occasion she was forced to be it. She shook her head because even though he was gone he still haunted her every day. Gabrielle got up and took a nice long hot shower trying to wash away any thoughts of Greg.

When she walked out, she noticed an envelope that looked like it had been pushed under the door. She rushed to the envelope and opened it up. There was money, a credit card with Lincoln's name on it, and a note that simply said, "I miss you." She snatched the door open but there was no one in the hallway. She walked back into the room and sat on the edge of the bed. She laid the money and card on the side table next to bed and reread the letter with a huge smile on her face. She imagined him saying those simple three words to her and melted onto her bed.

He misses me, she thought as she held on to the letter as if her life depended on it.

"I miss you too."

12
REBUKING DIABLOS

"Ok so we've gathered you all here to fill you in on the missing prostitute case that's been going on for almost six months." Lincoln felt like he wanted throw up as he listened to his captain speak. "Apparently there has been a shortage of hookers on the streets." The room broke into a fit of snickers all around. "Hey calm down this shit is not funny. I have the FBI talking about coming in to my house to find out why I can't account for the whores in this damn town!"

"But sir can a hooker even be missing? I mean they probably switched up avenues," one officer called out.

"Yeah I suggested the same thing, but we seem to have law abiding and family oriented prostitutes in the city of St. Louis because their families are looking for them. Hell some even have jobs calling in to report them missing." He exhaled deeply as he pinned up eight pictures of the women who had gone missing. "Now some of these go as far back as seven years."

"But sir, where do we even begin to find any information on a missing hooker from seven years ago?" Mike asked.

Lincoln started to fidget in his chair. Instantly sweat poured from his pores and nausea quickly consumed him, but he had to keep his meltdown in check so no one would notice how nervous he was. He looked at the pictures on the board and Monique's smile stared back at him. He felt a barrage of emotions come over him. Looking at her face stirred something in his soul.

*****

"Hey, we have to get it together." Lincoln looked around the dark room to see whose voice that was but he saw no one there. Lincoln sat rocking back and forth.

"Lincoln are you listening to me?" Lincoln just sat there in the corner mumbling to himself. "Lincoln we will make it through this. I'm here to help, just let me take over."

Lincoln stopped rocking and listened for the voice again. When he didn't hear it, he got up and turned on the light in the room. He was the only one there alive. Monique lay at his feet with blood surrounding her body.

"I'm sorry please forgive me." The sight of her almost sent him into a fit of tears again.

"No we are not going to cry anymore. Man up, we can't rewind the hands of time Lincoln."

Lincoln looked around to see who was talking but there was no one else in the room with him.

"Look at me Lincoln, look in the mirror." Lincoln turned to the mirror and was mortified by all the blood he was covered with. His eyes were bloodshot red and swollen.

"Who are you?"

"I am Zachariah."

Lincoln looked into mirror to make sure he saw his lips moving. As he got closer to the mirror, he asked again.

"Who are you?" He watched for his mouth to move again.

"I am Zachariah, I am you, and I am the will of the Lord your mother speaks of." Lincoln saw his own mouth moving but the voice was different. The baritone was too deep to be his own voice.

"Why are you here, where did you come from?" Lincoln put his face so close to mirror his lips almost rubbed against it when he spoke.

"I am here to help you and I came from you. I am you; I am a part of you that you tried to bury when you killed your mother. But I've always been here with you."

"And your name is Zachariah like my middle name?"

"Yes Lincoln. I am Zachariah, the will of Lord. The wrath of the Lord. I am here to help smite all the sinners from the earth and show them that the Lord is very unhappy with their wayward ways of living."

*****

"Well, Owens, all we can do right now is keep our ears to the ground, because we don't have any bodies to know if these people are really dead or even in trouble. However, with all the phones calls it's raised some red flags. So technically, we have no crime committed as of yet. I am just making you all aware of what's going on in your city." The officers chatted bringing Lincoln back to the current pressing situation.

"Damn, so what you think going on with the disappearance of all the prostitutes of St. Louis?" Mike asked Lincoln as they drove towards Mike's home.

"Hell if I know man. I just wish they would all just leave or disappear." Lincoln stared out the window as Mike stared at the back of his head. He didn't feel like talking at the moment. His nerves were shot and just wanted to be alone.

Mike didn't respond to what Lincoln had said because he was used to Lincoln making such harsh statements. He just shook his head and they rode in silence the rest of the way.

"Hey give me a little more time tonight, the wife is in heat," Mike laughed as he exited the car.

"A'ight be back in a little bit," Lincoln responded dryly.

Mike stood and watched Lincoln pull off. Normally he would have something smart to say. Mike noticed a change in his partner lately and hoped he was going to be alright. He had gotten used to Lincoln's episodes when he withdrew from people. He really wished Lincoln would go and talk to someone, but trying to convince him to talk to someone was like trying to get a cat to sit in water.

*****

Lincoln decided to visit a different hooker hang out that night because things were getting tight around his way. The local truck stops were another spot known to have a lot of prostitutes hanging around. Sure enough, he had hit the motherlode of whorism. It was nighttime so all the freaks and sex fiends were out in full force. He didn't know what he had stumbled upon but he could tell some real kinky things took place there.

Lincoln watched how the prostitutes truck hopped, going from one truck to the next. Lincoln had heard the truck drivers would keep bed and cots in the back of their trucks for when they needed to rest after hours of driving

"This is ridiculous my child."

"I know Mother, I'm trying," Lincoln gritted trying to control his anger.

"Well you're not trying hard enough. These people seem to be multiplying the second," Dorothy scoffed

"What do you want me to do, throw a bomb over there?" he asked sarcastically.

"I want you to fix it! Like the Lord has demanded of you dammit!"

Lincoln put his head down on the steering wheel. Sure enough, she would be his reason for an early death.

"Look you crazy bitch, didn't he say were we trying? Now back the fuck up." Zachariah hated Dorothy and didn't hide that fact at all.

"Oh it's you now huh? My son doesn't want to talk with me anymore I guess."

"You guessed right now go away."

"I want that one, you little ingrate." Dorothy pointed to a hooker that had just gotten out of the front of one of the eighteen-wheelers. She was smiling and wiping her mouth so anyone with eyes could figure out what she had just finished doing. She adjusted her skimpy dress and tried to pull it down a little, but it looked like it may have been washed one too many times and must have shrunk. She wore no stockings under the worn out dress and her pumps looked like the heels would break if she stepped on the smallest crack in the ground.

"Why her?" Zachariah had no problems with the woman she had chosen, he just wanted to know why she picked her. There were plenty of women roaming around so what made her stand out?

"Because that's who the Lord said should be punished."

"His will, my hand."

Chelsey walked towards the bathroom to clean herself as she counted the money she had made that night. She was happy she made her rent and even a little extra to pay the daycare that watched her 3-year-old son. She smiled at the thought of her son. He was the only reason she even still got out of bed. She had been on her own since she was 13, when her mother kicked her out for getting pregnant by her mother's boyfriend after he had raped her. She was now 17, back in school, and paying her way through life by selling her body.

She walked without a care in the world not watching her surroundings. Something she normally didn't do considering in her profession. It was necessary to keep your head on a swivel.

Lincoln watched her go into the bathroom and pulled his police car right outside the door. He got out and waited for her to exit.

"Shit," Chelsey cursed when she walked out and saw the police car in front of her. She didn't have time to be going to jail and using her hard-earned money to bond out or even worse, if the officer really wanted to be a jackass, he would just take the money she had earned that night. She turned around to go back in, and was met by Lincoln standing in her way.

"Look…"

Her sentence was stopped short as Lincoln shot the stun gun into her stomach. She dropped right where she stood. Lincoln pulled her into the car and pulled off slowly so he wouldn't draw any attention to himself.

"Dorothy," Zachariah said as he drove to his home, but she didn't respond to him.

"Dorothy I know you are there."

"Yes, Zachariah, I'm always here."

"Oh really, are you there when I am..."

"Don't you dare, absolutely not! I would never watch your perverted acts. You are a monster!" Dorothy yelled cutting off him off.

"Look at the pot calling the kettle black. Your denial is comical lady."

"You have some nerve the way you are raping these whoremongers."

"Look, lady, how long will we have to do this?"

"Son this wasn't a temporary assignment. This is a lifetime deal," she answered sincerely.

"I am not your son and he doesn't want to do this the rest of his life."

"Where is all this coming from? It's that woman he's been lusting over isn't it?" she spat.

"It could be her doing but you don't worry your crazy little head over that. I'm going to handle that. Lincoln just wants to be a normal person that goes to work and comes home to just sleep or go to movies. Simple shit, that's all."

"I knew she was going to be trouble, I do not approve of this relationship."

"Before you finish, no!" Zachariah shook his head at what he knew she was about to say. "He won't do it again." He laughed. "He loves this one even more than Monique and if you make him do that we would lose him forever. I won't let him do it. You and the Lord can go to hell."

"Blasphemy, you little ungrateful bastard! How dare you speak of the Lord in such a way?"

"Look just go away, this my alone time," Zachariah said as he stepped out of his car and began pulling Chelsey out of the backseat.

"It seems like you two need some time to think about your priorities."

"Whatever," Zachariah huffed as he threw Chelsey over his shoulder and kept walking ignoring Dorothy in the process. He was beyond frustrated at the way things were going. Zachariah knew his commitment was life long, but it seemed, as though Lincoln held hope that God would let him off the hook. But even finding love doesn't get you a get out of jail free card, and Zachariah planned to bring Lincoln back to reality.

When Chelsey opened her eyes, she was tied to what looked like a wooden bed with no mattress. She was naked and on her back, the only thing that was touching the makeshift bed was her ass, the rest of her was suspended in the air. The torture device known as The Rack was made out of a wooden frame with two ropes fixed at the bottom and the other two tied into the handle at the top. Zachariah sat in front of her, staring at her, going over what he was about to do in his head. He had never used The Rack but he couldn't wait to see the carnage in real life, instead of the You Tube videos of what people assumed it did in the medieval times.

"What is this?" Chelsey asked as she looked around trying to get a good look at the contraption she was in, it resembled something she had seen in a slave movie, where the slave owner had tied each of the slave's limbs to a horse. Then they would slap the horses on the ass so they could run in four different directions ripping the slave's limbs from their body.

"This is your judgment sinner. Are you ready to answer to the Lord for your sins?" He looked in her eyes in time to see tears running down the sides of her face.

"What the hell is this? Let me go you sick bastard!" She fought futilely against her restraints.

"You have been judged and it's time for the wrath of God to show you the error of your ways." Zachariah rose up slowly like a black cloud covering the sun. He examined her beautiful body as she struggled. Her chocolate quarter sized areoles stuck out like Hershey Kiss drops as her 34 D breasts jiggled.

"Please, what have I done to you? I have a son,

please don't do this!" she begged as she watched him circle her body like a predator stalking its next meal.

"All you whoremongers beg for your pitiful life and you only think of your kids when you're about to die," he scoffed at her. "Were you thinking of him when you were sucking and fucking those truck drivers?

"Yes, I was I only doing it to support him."

"Fuck that; take your trifling ass back to school. You people kill me. Too proud to work at McDonalds but will sell your body in the back alleys of every project to keep yourself in designer threads. Hell I even respect strippers more than you bottom feeders." He rolled his eyes at her.

"If you hadn't noticed I wasn't wearing anything designer," she yelled back at him.

Zachariah walked around to the end where her head was and picked up one of the gallons of water he had sitting behind The Rack, then he stood over her.

"What are you doing?"

"So put to death the sinful and earthly things lurking with in you." Zachariah began to pour the water on to her face. "Have nothing to do with sexual immorality, impurity, lust, and evil desires." Chelsey gagged and choked as she fought to keep the water from flooding her lungs. "Don't be greedy, for a greedy person is an idolater, worshiping the things of this world." He stopped pouring water, gripped the handle, and began twisting it pulling the ropes tight.

"Please mister don't do this!" Chelsey screamed as she felt her bones being pulled out of their sockets. The skin at her joints started to burn as it was being stretched to its limits. The pain that was radiating through her body, made her wish for death.

Zachariah continued twisting even as he heard her bones popping. He had never used that particular contraption and was quite pleased at what it did. He could to see her skin begin to tear around her shoulders and hips and wondered which one would rip apart first. Blood began to pour profusely from where the skin had begun to rip. The pain that showed in her eyes made his hollow soul smile. Chelsey's guttural screams were something he had never heard before.

"Because of these sins the anger of God is coming." He finished his prayer. With one last turn of the rod, he watched Chelsey's arms separate from her body. He looked on curiously, as she took her last breaths. A large puddle of blood had formed around her body, as it lay grotesquely disfigured.

Zachariah stared at her dead body lying there and didn't feel the gratification he normal would have felt after ridding the world of one more of its diseases.

13
SAVE ME

"I need to see you." Lincoln was on the verge of mental breakdown. He sat in his car staring at a building he had vowed years ago never to enter again. The office building that sat adjacent to his car was like a horror movie to him.

The St. Louis Children's Psychiatric Hospital was where the government made him relive everything his mother had put him through over and over again. They wanted him to sit and talk about it like they were talking about how blue the sky was and not how he had been tortured all his life.

The building itself had an ominous feel about it. If you had any hope when you entered the building, by the time you left all the life would be vacuumed from your soul. Children sat around staring at the puke green walls. Slobbering all over themselves, talking to no one, pacing back and forth with a twitch that most likely came from the medications they were on.

"Lincoln?" Dr. Langston questioned.

Dr. Melanie Langston had been Lincoln's childhood psychiatrist and hadn't heard from him in years. She would never forget him; his story gave her nightmares for weeks. The raspiness of his voice would send chills down anyone's spine if you heard it in the dark. She was a child psychiatrist and even though he was now grown up, she would never deny him help.

"Yes, it's me. Can I come in?" He sounded like he was on the verge of tears as if he was pleading with her to let him come see her.

"Yes, you can come in the morning." She looked at the clock and it was almost midnight. She liked to keep herself available for her clients at all times. She reasoned that mental breakdowns didn't have a time period for when they occurred.

"I need to see you now, please, don't make me go back to sleep." He was now in tears. Lincoln felt like he had a thousand pound weight sitting on his chest and it was making it hard for him to breathe. "I'm afraid she won't let me wake back up." He hadn't felt this way in years. When he was younger, he used to have severe anxiety attacks whenever someone mentioned his mother or his childhood. He would shake violently and it would feel as if someone wrapped a boa constrictor around his chest cavity. Sweat would pour from his pores and he wouldn't be able to stop the continuous flow of tears that would start.

"Ok Lincoln close your eyes and take in some deep breaths." Dr. Langston tried to calm him down remembering how bad his anxiety attacks would get; they were something she had never experienced before. He was in a class all on his own.

"I can't breathe." He rocked back and forth while hugging himself.

"Ok Lincoln we can meet at the office. I'm on my way."

Lincoln took another glance at the building of horrors and prayed it wasn't as bad as remembered. He could remember dreading going there as child, but now as an adult, he felt like he needed it for his survival.

Dr. Langston had no idea he was already waiting for her. He had jumped up out of his bed after a nightmare about his mother and called Dr. Langston. He didn't know what was going on with him; his emotions were all over the place lately. Usually, he would just call Jill and she would calm him down, but now he wanted real help. He was now ready to let go of his mother and take the steps to become a normal person. He knew it was going be like trying to push a bus up a wining, pothole filled hill, but he was willing to fight.

He watched as Dr. Langston pulled up to the curb in a shiny new BMW. He wondered if getting a BMW was the trendy thing to do after you become a doctor because every doctor he saw had one. She still looked the same as when he had last seen her. He watched her walk up to the door. She was a petite little lady with wide hips and big breasts. Her chocolate covered skin always made Lincoln think of a Milkyway. She wore her hair in a short wrap that fell just below her ears.

As Dr. Langston put her hand on the doorknob to go in, she felt a presence looming over her. She would have jumped but she could never forget the type of energy Lincoln brought when he came around. His presence always brought on a goose bumps type of feeling.

"Lincoln, I hope I haven't kept you waiting long." Dr. Langston turned the key not even looking at him as he stepped out of the shadows.

"No ma'am I just got here," he lied. He didn't want her to know he had been sitting outside her office for a few hours just thinking.

"Did you really, so that wasn't you sitting across the street?" Dr. Langston turned to smile at him as she ushered him in. No matter how creepy she thought he was, he was always nice and respectful to her. And behind all the scars, he still had a bright a smile, when he decided to show it.

"You got me Doc," he returned her smile.

"You pulled me out of my good slumber; let's not start out with lies. We are going to get to the nitty-gritty about some things tonight mister," Dr. Langston exclaimed.

"I'm sorry." He looked down at the floor. As he walked down the halls of the building, he could see it hadn't changed a bit. There wasn't the hustle and bustle of everyone running around due to the fact they were the only people there, but it still had the same smell and the same ugly puke green walls, lined with pictures of ugly old men. He assumed they used to work there or were the founders. He stood in the doorway of her office timidly, not sure of what he was about to do. It felt like once he stepped over the threshold of the office, there would be no turning back.

"Don't be sorry that's what I'm here for." She took off her charcoal grey pea coat and hung it on the brass hooks sprouting from the tall cherry coat hanger, revealing a black and white Adidas tracksuit. You could tell she dressed in a rush but she was still beautiful with her short hair pulled back into a little bushy ponytail.

"What, look, you call me at midnight this is what you gon' get," she chuckled.

"I ain't said nothing Doc." He laughed with her; he had never seen her out of her business attire. Her hips and ass stuck out stretching the seams of the tracksuit to its limits. She had the jacket zipped just enough to show a little cleavage.

"Now tell me what's going on." Dr. Langston pointed to the couch for him to lay down on as she sat in a chair across from the couch.

"I just want to be happy," Lincoln flopped down on the couch and closed his eyes.

"Well what's stopping you from being happy?"

"She won't leave me alone."

"When you say, she, are you referring to your mother, Dorothy?" Dr. Langston asked as she pulled out her notepad.

Lincoln paused for a few minutes before he answered. "Yes, I don't understand why she won't leave." He kept his eyes closed because he was ashamed and didn't want to see the way Dr. Langston was looking at him. He always thought people were looking down on him.

"Are you still holding on to her, because of what happened? Do you think maybe it's your conscious feeling guilty for killing her?"

"You know Doc, I never thought about it that way, but I don't feel guilty for what I did. It was her or me; she was trying to kill me when I killed her." For years, he felt guilty for what he had done, but Jill convinced him that he was not wrong. No mother should ever harm her child the way his mother did him.

"Ok let's rewind a little. What have you been doing lately? I haven't seen you in what, about five or six years?" She recalled the last time they had seen each other; he had gotten really upset when she brought up his mother and trying to get rid of her permanently. He wasn't ready to let her go then and he never came back again.

"I'm a police officer now, helping clean up the streets one day at a time." He shrugged his shoulders as if his job was nothing.

"Oh how is that going for you?" She looked up from her notebook to see his response.

"It has its perks." Dr. Langston could feel that there was something more to that remark but she wouldn't push just yet.

"Ok, is there a woman in your life, do you have a family yet?"

"Yes and no." He opened his eyes in time to catch Dr. Langston giving him a surprised look.

"I know right, who would want to be with me?" Lincoln felt a little hurt by her look of surprise. "But for some reason she's into me."

Dr. Langston could see the love in his eyes when he mentioned the young lady. She could tell his heart was smiling at that very moment.

"I didn't mean anything by that look. I was just surprised you let someone get close to you." She honestly never thought he would be able to have a normal life after what his mother had done to him. And the fact that he refused her help most of the time didn't help matters any either.

"I understand, I didn't want her to get close to me but she is forcing her way in and I don't want to stop her. I'm drawn to her. Like there is a magnetic force pulling me to her. I think of her every second of every hour. I only smile when I think of her.

"Have you told her about your past?"

"No, that's why I'm here. I don't know what to

do. Then there is my mother, how do I tell her my dead mother is haunting me?"

"Can I hypnotize you Lincoln?" She knew he wouldn't outright tell her what was going on but his subconscious may let her in.

"Sure if you think that will help any." He shrugged his shoulders not really believing it would work. He had seen people be hypnotized on TV and always thought they were faking.

"Ok then Lincoln I need you to relax." Dr. Langston watched as his shoulders fell lower, showing the sign that his muscles were totally relaxed. "Take in ten slow deep breaths."

Lincoln did as he was told to do. "What's this supposed to do Doc?"

"Just relax, Lincoln, I need you to imagine that you're standing in front of a black door. Do you see the door Lincoln?"

"Yes."

"That door is going to lead you to your mother."

"No I don't want to go in Doc." She could see in his face that he was really scared to go to that part of his mind.

"It's ok. I'm here with you, just open the door. We have to see why she is still here."

"Ok." Lincoln put his hand on the doorknob and slowly turned it.

"Are you in Lincoln? What do you see?"

"I thought he got rid of you years ago. How we end up back in this shithole" Dr. Langston could see Lincoln's lips moving but it was a different voice.

"Excuse me?"

"Why is he here again? What have you been poisoning my boy's brain with? You know he's vulnerable now a days."

"Who are you?" Dr. Langston asked shocked at what was happening.

"So he hasn't told you about me yet, huh?" Zachariah asked as he turned and sat so he was face to face with Dr. Langston. His smirk gave her chills.

"I'm afraid we haven't gotten that far. What did you say your name was again?"

"I am the will of the Lord. The wrath of the Lord. I am the hand that smites the sinners from the world, I am Zachariah."

"Oh really, and who gave you these names?"

"Again why are we here? What has he told you?"

"He hasn't told me anything as of yet. We were hoping his mother could enlighten us on why she is still hanging around. But he hasn't mentioned you."

"Oh really?"

"Yes, Lincoln says she won't leave, and he doesn't know why. Why do you think Dorothy is still here?"

"According to her she will always be here and she's been sent back to make sure he stays true to his promise to the Lord. Or some rigmarole to that nature." He threw his hands in the air in an exaggerated gesture.

"What promise is that sir?"

"You really think you know your sweet little innocent Lincoln, don't cha?" Zachariah looked at her peculiarly.

"What do you mean by that? No I do not pretend that I know everything."

"You people are funny; this whole thing is a crock of shit! You know absolutely nothing," Zachariah scoffed at Dr. Langston. "People pay you money for you to sit and ask a millions questions and still get nowhere. This mess doesn't work. The Lord is the only way to rid yourself of your sins. God is the only way."

"I'm sorry you feel that way. If this is a crock as you say, why did you come?"

"Because, as always, I am here to make sure our good ole boy Lincoln keeps his fucking mouth closed."

"So you are afraid he may tell me some deep dark secret that you want to keep hidden?"

"Look, dig this here Doc; I wouldn't give a fat fuck about what he told you, but I know you people are all the same talking about doctor patient confidentially and all that other bullshit. But the minute you muthafuckas get some TV worthy info, you become private informants and shit."

"You watch too much TV young man." Dr. Langston chuckled at his account of her profession. She had heard all the stereotypical scenarios of her job but his version was a bit askew.

Zachariah stared at her for what seemed like an eternity to Dr. Langston. Silence filled the room and the tension had risen so high that she had started to become uncomfortable.

Dr. Langston had begun unconsciously fidgeting was the zipper on her jacket. She felt her palms getting clammy. It didn't seem as though Zachariah was looking at her. It almost felt like he was looking into her trying to find something within her soul.

"You know you are just as useless now as you were when he was a child."

Dr. Langston paused before she responded. She noticed the voice was different this time.

"And can I ask who you are?" Dr. Langston asked. She had a feeling about who she was talking to but she wanted to hear her say it

"You know damn well who I am sinner. Let's not play with each other's intelligence or lack thereof." Dorothy leaned back on the couch and smirked.

Dr. Langston's mind was in a whirlwind full of questions. She had studied these kinds of cases and seen plenty of episodes of "Criminal Minds" on multiple personality disorders. In her ten years as a child psychiatrist, she had never run across a case like Lincoln's.

"Should I call you Dorothy?"

"That is my name, but I'd prefer if you didn't call me anything whoremonger." Dr. Langston looked into Lincoln's eyes and saw nothing but emptiness. Not the sparkle that twinkled when he spoke of his new found love.

"Why won't you leave Lincoln alone?"

"Because I need my son to know I am a part of him and will always be. I am going absolutely nowhere. He made a vow and I am going to make sure he's keeping his part of the deal."

"Ok." Dr. Langston paused for moment to try to find the right words to form a question she had wanted to ask for years. "Why did you do the hurtful things you did to Lincoln when he was child."

"I don't know what you are talking about. Lincoln and I had a wonderful relationship."

Dr. Langston was confused at first until she remembered his mother was schizophrenic and had no knowledge of the things she had done to Lincoln. That revelation also let her know that she had passed on her schizophrenia to Lincoln; he just didn't know it yet.

"Ok well can you tell me what happened between you and Lincoln's father?"

"Look sinner you just leave my son alone or I will bring the wrath of God down on you so hard you will pray for death!"

Dr. Langston watched Lincoln blink his eyes repeatedly. He looked around as if he was just waking up from a long slumber.

"What happened? Did it work?" Lincoln asked as he sat up.

"Yes…It did. Your mother and a male spoke to me." She watched for his reaction.

"Wait you talked to Zachariah?" Lincoln looked worried.

"Yes."

"And Dorothy spoke to you too?" She nodded her head up and down. "Did you see them?"

"No I didn't see them, they spoke through you."

"Huh, how is that possible?"

"I believe you have a Dissociative Identity Disorder, in other words, split personalities."

"Get the fuck out of here." He couldn't believe what he was hearing. She had to be crazy. "How is that?"

"When a young child suffers from the kind of trauma that you went through in your childhood their mind can split."

"You can stop it right there Doc. I am not the male version of Sybil so stop reaching. I've never had moments where I don't remember what I've done. I am aware of everything I do!"

This was very reason why Lincoln had stopped

coming to see her years ago because she tried to say he was schizophrenic like his mother. He knew something was wrong with him but she was reaching for the stars and he wasn't having it. Sure, he knew about Zachariah but his mother was just a voice he couldn't seem to ignore. No, he wasn't and no one was going to make him feel like a psychotic nut case.

"So you were aware that you were talking to me as your mother and Zachariah?" He was in denial and had been in denial for years about his condition.

"You had me hypnotized there is no telling what happened while I was under. But when I am conscious I am aware of all my doings." He was heated all over again and wished he could have taken her to his shed to teach her a lesson for fucking with his head. He knew deep down inside something was wrong, and that it wasn't normal for anyone to have another personality, but he refused to be labeled.

"Ok, Lincoln, no need to get upset. I was just suggesting that was the reason your mother isn't leaving. She said she would always be a part of you. Do you know why she said that?" She really wanted to help him but he had to get past his denial. She now knew for sure he had split personality. She hoped he would let her get to the bottom of things once and for all.

Lincoln once again stared at Dr. Langston for a while before he answered her. His mother had always told him she would be a part of him and would never leave no matter what he did. And for the doctor to repeat that to him, he knew something had transpired while he was under hypnosis.

"Look, Doc, I don't know why that was said to you." He took a deep breath. "I have to go, I'll be back soon." He felt defeated all over again. It was true; she was never going to leave him alone. He would never have an happily ever after with Gabrielle, or any woman for that matter.

14
DOROTHY'S STORY

"Look I'm sorry I never told you I was married but I was just having fun with you and didn't see the need." Charles let out a long sigh waiting for Dorothy's response. He had no time for her nonsense. He knew she was a bit off but she was going overboard with her antics lately and he wanted to be done with her.

Dorothy had gotten on some fatal attraction type of shenanigans. She had started following him home, calling his phone all times of the night.

When she had first found out about his wife, she had gone ballistic. She sent messages threatening to kill him and his wife in their sleep. She'd gone as far to throw herself down a flight of stairs to get attention from him, but he paid her no attention and told her to pull herself together and put on her big girl panties.

"What do you mean you were having fun?" Her eyes shrunk down to mere slits and zoomed in on him as if she was an eagle about to snatch up its prey. "You screwed me every night, made me promises, and told me you loved me!" Dorothy was irate and he was about to feel her wrath. He had played with her emotions.

Charles stood almost statuesque, looking smug like he couldn't be touched but she was about to show him differently. The once beautiful brown eyes she had adored now reminded her of a couple of snake eyes. His cheekbones that were once perfectly positioned on his face now resembled the Joker's ugly grin. Even though he towered over her five-foot four frame with his six-foot three inches the inferno burning within her made her feel seven feet tall.

"Are you fucking serious? When did I tell you I loved you?" He looked at her as if she had grown two heads in a matter of minutes. He was used to her crazy antics and told her on many occasions to go get checked out, but she would never go. The constant praying, pacing, seeing, and hearing shit that wasn't there had started to get on his nerves and he was through with it all.

Charles wanted out and no matter what she said; he was gone with the wind. He had awakened one morning after hearing someone talking. When he'd gotten out of bed to check the situation out, he had found Dorothy in the corner of the bathroom praying on her knees. Her hair was everywhere and she was naked scratching at her arms and legs. Red welts covered her body. He was all for people praying but she was begging for forgiveness for her weakness of the flesh and telling God that she would kill herself for his mercy. He snuck out of the house that night only coming back to get his belongings he had left when he was in a rush.

"You son of bitch!" she screamed. "You think you can just go around fucking women and stomping on their hearts without a care in the world?" The look on his face was making her skin crawl. He had this sneaky grin plastered on his face as if he knew a secret that no one else knew but him. His freshly shaved head shined under the moonlight that shown through the window resembling a shiny bowling ball. His clothes were a little wrinkled because they had just gone a few round of sweaty sex.

"Look get rid of it. Do us both a favor. You don't want to pass along what it is that has you fucked up in head to the poor baby." He laughed because he couldn't believe she was pulling the pregnancy card on him. He had been there done that plenty of times and she was no different from the rest, or so he thought.

"So, me and my child mean absolutely nothing to you," she said it more in a matter of fact tone than a question.

Dorothy stood there in her baby blue silk teddy. Her temperature had gone up a thousand degrees. Sweat dripped down under her breasts and the back of her thighs. Her palms began to itch with anticipation. She paced back and forth talking to herself. Rambling about sinners and people having to pay for their sins.

Charles watched her closely as he inched slowly toward the bedroom door. He could see a storm brewing in her head. He'd done a lot of dirt with too many women to count. Never did he think Karma would come back for payback in the form of an assuming homely woman like Dorothy.

"I know that I am being punished for the sins of fornicating with you. But what will be your punishment?" She stared at him intently trying to figure out the direction God wanted her to go in. They were both sinners but she wouldn't be the only one feeling the wrath of God. "Won't you pray with me?"

"Bitch you done lost the last little bit of your mind that you had left." Charles took a couple more steps towards the door so he could make a quick getaway.

"Just come pray with me and God will forgive you for your sins against me and your wife." The thought of him having a wife seared her insides and made her want to throw up.

Charles had sold her a dream that was now a nightmare. He had told her he loved her and would be with her forever. Only thing about that was Dorothy was the only one who didn't know she was just dreaming. In all reality, he only came at night to visit her. They never talked and he never answered his phone for her. The only truth to their relationship was that she was pregnant and he never told her he was married. Dorothy had created a wonderland of love in her head that no one else was allowed entrance to.

"I think it's time for me to just leave, I really feel like you need time to think. I don't know what's gotten into you lately, but you really need to get help." His bowels had shifted and he felt like he would shit his pants at any given second.

Charles wasn't really a tough guy at all. He was a smooth talker that loved to get pussy any way he could get it. Charles watched her intently making sure he could see her hands at all times. The glossed over look in her eyes made him wish he had packed his gun. He was in the living room with no weapon in sight. Her deathly gaze was burning a hole through his soul. He could truly see that tempestuous line between love and hate in her eyes.

"Yeah I think it's time for you to go also." The look she was giving him let him know he could take that innuendo a couple of different ways.

"Look, let's not make this bigger than what it is."

"Really? I'm standing here telling you I'm pregnant, and then you tell me you're done with me!" She looked at him as she walked over to the fireplace where all of her mother's snow globes were strategically placed. "I poured out my heart out to you. Then you tell me to get rid of my baby?" She picked up one of the snow globes that had Santa Claus in a sleigh being led by his seven reindeer.

"Look, now, it doesn't have to be this way." He could tell things were about to take a turn for the worse and jetted towards the door. As soon as he turned the knob, she launched the snow globe like a pitcher in the National Baseball League. The sound of the snow globe connecting with the back of his head sounded like someone had just hit a home run out of Busch Stadium.

Charles fell to the floor dazed. He could see her moving around the kitchen frantically like she was looking for something. Next thing he knew, she was charging towards him like a raging bull. Her eyes resembled that of person on a psychotic break. The closer she got to him, the bigger the knife she had in her hand seemed to get. Panic set in as she kneeled down beside him. She already had blood on her. He tried to look to see where the blood was coming from. For a moment, he prayed it was a sign of a miscarriage.

"You were just going to leave me high and dry huh?" Dorothy let out a wicked chuckle as she lowered the knife to his neck. "Run off into the sunset with your wife and kids?" She shook her head as she applied pressure, drawing blood. He could tell her mind had totally checked out. Her realm of reality stretched far beyond what he could have imagined.

Charles watched her intently through blurry eyes, waiting on her attention to shift to anything but her putting that knife through his neck. She closed her eyes as if she was in deep thought. Charles took that as his cue. He brought the snow globe up and smashed it against her head. It had rolled next to him after it connected with his head. The hit caused her to fall back and in the process, slice through the soft flesh of the skin on his neck. That wouldn't stop him from getting up and running to his car though. He got out of there like his pants were on fire. Luckily, for him, the cut wasn't deep enough to cause any major problems. He just wanted to get away and never see her again. And that's exactly what he did, he never saw her again. He moved his family out of town with no forwarding address.

*****

"So you are pregnant by a married man?" Dorothy's mother Tina looked at her pitifully then shifted her eyes to the floor in shame. Tina was very disappointed in her only child.

"Yes ma'am," Dorothy admitted. She was so embarrassed she couldn't even look in her father's direction.

"I know we've taught you better than this. Threw your life away and for what? Is he going to help you?" her mother chastised.

"He wants nothing to do with me or the baby," Dorothy cried.

"Well I'm with him, he's right, because we don't want anything to do with you and your child either!" her father yelled.

"Ed, this is not the time!" her mother yelled.

"The hell it isn't!"

"How is she going to raise a child when she has issues of her own?"

"Daddy I can do it," Dorothy whispered not believing her own pleas.

"You don't have a choice because you got to get the hell out of here. I want no parts of this shit!" He was hurt and couldn't believe his baby girl had thrown her life away for a no good married man.

"Ed you are not putting my daughter out into the streets!"

"You can go with her; maybe she'll teach you how to get a married man to fuck you too!" He stormed out of the room.

"I'm sorry."

"No, Momma, it's ok, I'll get out." Dorothy's eyes were filled tears. She had not a clue as to what she was going to do. Her family had disowned her and Charles wanted no parts of her either.

The next day Dorothy's father moved all her belongings to the family house they owned by the lake. He had an automatic draft sent to a bank account that he had set up for and never looked back. He wouldn't leave her completely destitute but he wanted her out of his life. She was a disgrace to the family.

After that, Dorothy's sickness only got worse. With her not knowing, she was sick and no one was around to help her. She sank deeper and deeper into her insanity.

15
HELP ME HELP US

"Hello is Officer Donaldson in today?" Gabrielle looked around the police station hoping to spot Lincoln walking past. She hadn't talk to him in a days and it was driving her crazy. She needed to see him and hear his voice. The sight of him made her heart melt and she really needed that uplift at the moment. Even though Greg was gone, he still haunted her thoughts, consumed her daydreams, and was the reason for her night terrors. She would sit at the police station until his shift started or ended if that's what she had to do.

"Let me check," a receptionist answered. Gabrielle looked the receptionist over and had to bite her tongue to keep from laughing. The receptionist had a bottom row of gold teeth, and her lips painted a bright purple looked like they could suck the skin off an alligator's tail. Her eyebrows were thick and black; they looked like they had been drawn on with a magic marker. Gabrielle could barely look the ghetto queen in the eyes for fear of them coming to life and jumping on her, they resembled tarantulas.

Gabrielle unconsciously ran her hands along her

maxi dress to make sure everything was still looking good and that she wasn't looking like the travesty sitting in front of her. She had pinned her hair up in into a French roll and sported a long white maxi dress. She looked beautiful but the way Greg had beat up on her self-esteem she was never sure of how she looked. She would think she was looking pretty and he would shoot her right in the heart with hurtful words letting her know he did not approve of her attire for the day. He spewed so much hatred towards her that she almost became immune to it.

"Excuse me ma'am," the receptionist called to Gabrielle.

"Yes," she turned in excitement covered her face.

"He's not in today ma'am; would you like to leave a message?" In an instant, Gabrielle's smile faded. With every word the ghetto receptionist uttered, her spirits were crushed.

"No thank you I'll catch him some other time." Gabrielle walked away feeling defeated for the moment but she was determined to make him love her.

*****

"Mister what do you want with me?" Zachariah's latest mark asked, as she stood naked, chained to the wall of his shed. She looked around the spacious shed with blurry vision. With all the tools hanging and laying around it, appeared to be a normal garage. That is until her eyes zeroed in on all the wooden contraptions he had strategically placed throughout the cement covered space. She figured she had been drugged because her body felt weak and she could barely hold her head up straight.

"I want you to repent sinner," Zachariah stated calmly. When he spotted her getting out of one of her customer's cars, he pulled up in a beat up car that he kept in the garage. He had told her he wanted to get some head and she agreed not knowing she was getting into to the car with the Reaper reincarnate. That day he had to use his undercover car because he was off work, but sinners never stopped sinning so his duties needed to be completed.

When she went down to place him in her mouth, he pulled out his stun gun and tazed her.

"What have I done to you? Please let me go," she pleaded. "I promise not to tell anyone." Her body hung flaccidly against the wall. Had it not been for the chains she would have fallen to the over bleached cement floor. She struggled with the restraints almost getting one arm free. She had small delicate wrists and didn't mind breaking them to get free.

Seeing what she doing, Zachariah quickly grabbed the cattle prod and jammed it into her side sending high volts of electricity into her nervous system.

"Don't fuck with me," Zachariah gritted. "What

is your name sinner?" He didn't want to hear any of her pleas. She had been chosen and there was nothing he could do to save her. He stared at her and wondered why she was out selling her body. He often wondered what life choices they had made or what situations forced them into the lifestyles they were living, when he was looking into the eyes of his victims. He would never understand how such beautiful women had to stoop to sell their bodies on the streets to survive. Sure, everything costs, but a woman's body is like a priceless Egyptian gemstone and shouldn't be disgraced in the back alleys behind crack houses.

He watched as tears ran freely down her face but his heart was hollow so if she was looking for any sympathy, she was barking up the wrong tree.

"Tabatha Williams, please sir I have children," she cried as Zachariah studied her milky white flesh. She only had a landing strip of bright red curly pubic hair on her vagina. Her perky C cup breasts with quarter-sized areolas taunted him to suckle on them. He licked his lips as he thought about what they would taste like on his tongue.

"Where are your children?" Zachariah questioned raising an eyebrow.

"They are with my mother." She shifted her gaze so she wasn't looking him in the eyes. She was truly embarrassed by her relationship with her children. She often told people she didn't have any kids to avoid explaining why she no longer had custody of them.

"How long has it been since you've seen your children?"

She looked down to the ground. She hadn't seen her kids in years. Her mother wouldn't let her see them while she was still on drugs and running the streets. She hadn't always been hooked on drugs. However, one night of partying had changed her whole life. Someone had laced her joint with crack and with her being new to smoking at the time, the funny smell that coated the air didn't ring any alarms. She'd thought the tingling, numb feeling radiating through her body was a normal part of getting high. It only took her a few months to lose everything, her three children, home, and job. Ever since then she had been running the street trying to stay alive and chasing that ultimate high, but Zachariah was about to make her wish she had died way back then.

"I said, when the last time you saw your children was?" he yelled as he grabbed her face so she was looking at him. His eyes shrunk into slits and his brown eyes had turned black as he shot daggers at her with his eyes.

"Fuck you!" she spit in his face. He wiped it off calmly, walked over to the counter that he had all his special tools sitting on, and picked up his toy that he had recently made. He smiled wickedly when he picked it up. When he had found the medieval torture device online and decided to duplicate it, he couldn't wait to use it. The breast ripper was a metal claw that pierced the flesh of the breast. Lincoln duplicated everything in the picture down to the woman being chained to the wall. During the medieval era, the punisher would clamp the claw around the woman's breast and pull forcibly, shredding the woman's breast to pieces. Zachariah loved the way Lincoln's mind worked because he had handmade and picked each and every one of the devices in their little torture chamber in the woods. Lincoln took notice of the fact that there were plenty of ancient Chinese and medieval torture devices made especially for woman and he didn't have a problem with bringing them into the twenty-first century.

Zachariah turned around with a Dr. Evil smile on his face. Tabatha watched his every move wondering what the claw looking thing did. A million different scenarios played out in her head but she never once thought about was actually going to happen.

"And upon her forehead a name was written, a mystery, Babylon the great, mother of harlots, and the abomination of the earth." Zachariah paused as he placed the claw around her breast. "Have nothing to do with sexual immorality, impurity, lust, and evil desires. Don't be greedy, for a greedy person is an idolater, worshipping the things of this world. Because of these sins, the anger of God is coming."

"Wait a minute, please don't do this!" She panicked once she saw what he was about to do. She winced once the claw clamped down into the soft, meaty flesh of her breast. "Ple…" She didn't get to finish her plea because Zachariah had yanked the claw down shredding the meat of her breast in a swift motion. Horrible spine tingling screams erupted throughout the shed. She withered around in pain and shook the chains violently as her body went into convulsions. The shock to her system was so fierce that the air in her lungs ceased to exist.

"You sinners are the reason for the world being the way it is." Her body hung limp up against the wall. "I am the will of the Lord and his wrath will be felt."

He placed the clamp around her other breast and pulled forcefully, shredding that one also. He admired his handiwork as the meat and skin of her breasts hung like ropes on a mop. Thinking of something new, he grabbed a bag of salt from the corner of the shed. He slowly poured the salt making sure that the open area on her was covered in the salt. She shrieked out loud then passed out from shock. He let her hang there slowly bleeding to death as he cleaned up the area.

His mind had drifted to Lincoln and Gabrielle and how he would be able to get rid of her without losing Lincoln in the process.

The chains moving behind him caught his attention and brought him back to his current situation. He looked over his shoulder and could see Tabatha's near death limbs twitching. He decided to end her misery, grabbed a screwdriver, and walked hastily over to her; he pulled her head back so he was looking at her face. Slowly, she opened her eyes and looked up at him. Without any hesitation, he jammed the screwdriver into her left eye repeatedly until he was covered in blood and her body was no longer twitching.

*****

Gabrielle had been sitting around all day waiting for Lincoln to come by or even call, but to no avail. He still never showed up and it left her confused. She couldn't understand why he would help her only to leave her alone in the world. Didn't he know she needed him? Didn't he know she craved his touch and his presence was like oxygen to her lungs? She got up from the loveseat she had been sitting on and went to turn her bath water off. The sweet smell of vanilla filled the room's air and relaxed her senses. As she slid in, the hot water made her cringe a little but that didn't stop her from taking her whole body down under the water. When she brought her head out of the water, she heard the TV on.

She sat up quickly to make sure the sounds were coming from the other side of the bathroom door and not next-door. She looked around frantically for something to put on and for a weapon. Fear gripped her nerves. She had watched enough of her favorite show "Criminal Minds" to know that women were always killed and tortured getting out of the bathtub and she didn't want to make the news naked.

She threw on the complimentary robe and stormed into her room only to find Lincoln sitting on the edge of the bed shirtless watching ESPN. She wanted to run and jump onto his lap but she chose not to.

"What brings you by?" she asked with an

attitude. She let her eyes roam over his upper torso. His scars were beautiful to her. She knew there was nothing she could do to heal those scars, but she wanted desperately to help him heal the ones on his heart. She didn't know how he had become everything to her; she had awakened one morning with an overwhelming feeling of needing him in every way possible.

"I came to see you." He had been wondering what she was doing, was she thinking of him, did she miss him as much as he missed her. "I missed you." He smiled as he looked up into her eyes. She looked beautiful standing there dripping wet with her wet hair stuck to her face. He watched as the anger slowly disappeared from her face. She wanted to pout and keep up her attitude but he had sucker punched her. She wasn't expecting him to say that.

Slowly, he rose from the bed and stalked towards her backing her up until he had her pinned between him and wall. Her breaths became shallow as he stared into her eyes. It looked as though he could see clear through to her soul. He could see the flames of lust burning within her eyes. Lincoln knew she wanted him just as much as he wanted her. Gently, he pulled her face into his and pressed his lips up against hers. As his tongue did a sultry dance in her mouth, her knees almost gave out. The ache in her pussy was unbearable. She needed him to fill her up and work her over real good right there up against the wall. He let his hands slide lazily down her face and neck letting them rest on her breasts. As he massaged her hard nipples through the bathrobe, she let out a soft moan.

Gabrielle let her hands roam all over his body until her hands rested on his hard dick. His width alone scared her but when she couldn't find the end of it she knew she was in trouble. Lincoln undid the tie in her robe breaking her concentration.

"Don't worry, I'll be gentle." He had felt her body tense up when she felt his pole, but he wanted to assure her that he would never do anything to hurt her. Grabbing her by the ass, he slid her body up the wall until she was face to face to with him. She wrapped her legs around his waist like a baby monkey clinging to its mother. He reached under her and undid his pants letting them fall to the floor; next went his boxer briefs. His dick was hard as steel. He had told himself that he wasn't going to have sex with her, but the look in her eyes told him she needed it as much as he did. His sanity rested on her shoulders and she didn't even know it. Slowly and gently, he slid her down onto his hard pole taking into consideration that her husband wasn't as endowed as he was.

"Ssssss," she hissed as she went further and further down on to his pole. She dug her nails into his chest drawing blood. She hoped that she would get used to his girth and start to enjoy it. The searing pain that was going through her hot box was intense. It felt like she was being split in two, but she wouldn't dare ask him to stop, the intensity in his eyes let her know he needed this, and she would give him all of her if that's what it would take to keep him with her.

Lincoln had to bite down on her shoulder and suck hard to keep from screaming out; she was so tight and wet. He was used to having to lube up with other women, but not with Gabrielle, she was ready, hot, and moist. Once he felt her walls relax around his shaft slowly, he went in and out of her. She held on for dear life not wanting the moment to end.

"You okay?" he asked as he stroked her and sucked on her neck. He wasn't all the way in and hadn't expected to get as much in as he had, but her love tunnel accepted him and kept a good grip so he wouldn't go anywhere. He inhaled her scent burning the smell into his memory.

"Umm ye…ssssss." It took her a minute to get that whole word out. He was hitting spots she didn't even know she had. He gripped her ass, walked over to the bed, and laid down on top of her without slipping out of her pussy. She gasped when she felt him go deeper. He was hitting her with the death stroke. Both had been dreaming of that night and neither could have imagined it would be that good.

Her body was so soft under his touch if felt like his body was gliding against wet silk. He felt goose bumps spread across her flesh as he placed soft kisses all over her neck and collarbone. Her moans were singing a beautiful melody in his ear that he wanted to put on repeat. He pulled out without warning and spread her legs wide as he slid down her body until he was facing her pussy. As soon as he put his hot mouth on her clit, she came so hard the explosion that had just happened in her hot box took her breath away. Lincoln sucked on her clit hard but gently, making her orgasm last longer.

At this point, Gabrielle was moaning, screaming, and trying to run because he wasn't letting go of her love button. Once he figured out what she liked he wasn't going to let go until she passed out or waved the white flag. She felt another orgasm coming on and once it hit her, it set her soul on fire as her body locked. She couldn't move or breathe. Lincoln was face deep going to work on her pussy trying to let her know how he felt about her, because he would never be able to say it in words, so he decided to let his body do the talking for him

When he felt her body loosen up, he rose up with his face glistening with her juices. She pulled his face down to hers and licked her essence off his face as he slid back in. They made love in every position that night, taking both of their feelings and multiplying them by a thousand.

16
MY PAST IS MY FUTURE

"Look ma'am you are under arrest for solicitation. Now shut the fuck up before I make it resisting arrest also," Mike barked at the elderly prostitute. He arrested her almost every week for trying to sell pussy outside of the police station. Some days he thought she just needed a place to sleep for the night, so he obliged her most of the time. That day, she had swung on him but her equilibrium was off because of all the alcohol she had consumed, so she missed his face by a mile.

"Man listen. I ain't tried to sell nobody shit. These little knucklehead negros wouldn't know what to do with this sweet old pussy if they taught a class on how to handle the pussy! You better ask about me," she boasted and patted her crotch while humping the air. Mike figured there was a dust storm going on under the multi-colored jump suit. She wasn't a bad looking lady but he could tell the years on the streets had been hard on her by the dark rings around her eyes, splotchy skin, and toothless smile.

*****

Pauline had started out prostituting against her young will at the tender age of 8 years old. She wasn't put out on the streets to stand with the older more seasoned women. No, her mother preserved her sweet innocence and beauty for the wealthy perverts who liked little children. Most of the perverts didn't care whether it was a boy or girl. They just liked to watch the virtuousness fade from the adolescent's face.

Pauline's mother charged 2,000 dollars a pop for Pauline's virtue, and to make sure her daughter preserved her vaginal tautness she limited Pauline's clientele to two men per day. However, if a lady wanted to partake also, her mother would oblige figuring that there would be no penetration during their little experience.

Pauline wasn't thrown out on her own until she was fourteen and too old for the depraved souls that lusted after the essence of young children. By then her mother was so gone off the drugs that she no longer looked at Pauline as her daughter, she only saw dollars signs when she looked at the young girl. Poor Pauline was merely an ends to a means.

Pauline found herself homeless and selling her

body for anything, she could get her hands on. At that age, she could get any price she asked, but as the old saying goes the rest was history.

"I know Miss Pauline; I heard you got the sweetest honey pot west of the Mississippi." Mike laughed. She had been selling ass since before he was born and yes, it was true he had heard she had the meanest head and pussy around in her earlier years. Now, he wouldn't be surprised if her hot box was now colder than a frozen TV dinner. He grimaced at the thought.

"You better act like you know then nigga." She snaked her neck to make sure he knew she was serious. Mike looked at her. "Yeah I called you a nigga, black folk ain't the only niggas in the world!" she capped. "Before everyone got sensitive the dictionary said that a nigga meant ignorance, a lack of knowledge. And I done met plenty white, chinamen, and black folk that should wear the word with much pride. Because these are the most ignorant days of all my life!"

"Book her please," Mike laughed as he addressed an officer sitting behind a desk also laughing at the exchange.

"Say Officer Mike!" she called to him, Mike turned to look at her. "I'm trying to guide you into the light; you can't avoid the sunshine forever." She pointed to her crotch area and laughed as they pulled her away. "Don't cheat cha self, treat cha self. I'll have you call home to the missus saying you ain't never coming home!" she continued her rant as she was pulled down the hall.

Mike walked away still laughing at the old lady. She had been a barrel of laughs. However, his smile faded at the thought of the person who had been out hurting the prostitutes of St. Louis. What if the murderer ever got ahold of Miss Pauline, he would definitely be heart broken. She was considered one of his regulars and was like the drunk aunt that always clowned at the family gatherings. Even though she was a prostitute, Mike understood where she was coming from. One night when Mike had arrested her she had told him her whole life story. He was in tears when she was done and looked at her in a totally different light.

He walked up to the board that had all the missing prostitutes on it and studied all of their faces. To him, it didn't matter what your profession was, you didn't deserve to die alone. He felt like their families should have some kind of closure.

"Man why you be messing with that old lady?" Lincoln walked up to Mike and looked at the board too. He looked around at all the pictures and smiled inside because one by one he and Zachariah were getting rid of the infestation of the whores of the world, or at least in the city of St. Louis.

"Who Miss Pauline? That old lady crazy as hell. She just needed somewhere to sleep tonight." He shrugged his shoulders as he rubbed the beard he had been growing for the last few months.

"Um hm I bet. You tapped that yet?" Lincoln laughed again.

"Ha ha you're a real funny guy I see." Mike

looked at Lincoln then turned his attention back to the board. Lincoln watched Mike as he stared at all the pictures on the board. He wished he could read his mind. He prayed he wouldn't have to kill his only friend in the world to keep his surreptitious life concealed.

"Man what's up with you and ole girl?" Mike turned to see a cheese eating grin spread across Lincoln's face. "Aww man you finally got cha some huh?"

"Man I ain't about to tell you about my sex life."

"Since when? Get the fuck out of here. I have to screw the same box every night. I'm gon' live vicariously through you," Mike laughed.

"Not this time you won't fool. Let's get out of here man." Lincoln walked away trying to get away from Mike for a second. He knew Mike wasn't going to let up on the situation.

*****

"Stop over there so I can get me a something to drink," Mike told Lincoln as they came to a stop sign at the end of the hoe strip they patrolled.

"That's the pig I was telling you about Daddy!" Lincoln heard someone say as he was walking out of the store drinking his peach soda. He looked around to see who they were talking about. By the way, Mike had gotten out of the car, and was rushing toward him; he knew they were talking about him.

"What the fuck is y'all on?" Mike asked the whore and her pimp that had just walked up on Lincoln.

"My hoe tells me you been coming around here a lot lately. And that you might know about my missing bitch's whereabouts," the pimp stated smoothly.

"Fuck outta here, this my fucking beat. And you better back the fuck up before I embarrass yo' ass in front of yo' bitches," Lincoln threatened. Lincoln looked the old school pimp up and down and couldn't believe he had on a dark purple silk suit like he was on his way to a player's ball or some shit. His eight gold teeth shined under the streetlight and his beer breath smelled as if he had just sucked on a shitsicle. He was high yellow with silky smooth skin, and no facial hair giving him a baby face effect. However, looking in his eyes, one could tell the years had been rough on him. Mike stood right beside Lincoln with his hand resting on his gun.

"A'ight, slick, hands up don't shoot," the pimp said and threw his hands in mock surrender.

"Ain't nobody gon' shoot yo' dumb ass! But you and this big headed ass Muppet better scram before I pull her bottom lip over her head!"

"No nigga you need to tell me what you did with Tinka. You chased her down and I ain't seen her since!"

Lincoln's jaw muscles clenched tight to keep him from saying something he was going to regret.

He couldn't believe he didn't see this Smurf looking bitch the night he had taken the he/she. Lincoln had heard the trick Tinka was leaving call her that before he pulled off. Now he stood here with Smurfette accusing him of kidnapping in front of his partner. He wanted to snatch her ass by her nappy blue hair that looked like it had seen better day's years ago. She was five foot eight and shaped like Patrick from the cartoon Sponge Bob Squarepants. Her belly flap looked as if it were forming a body of its own on the front of her it stuck out so far. She wore a dingy gray dress that stopped just below her ass and looked like it had been black once upon a time. She had big bug eyes and a set of lips that looked like they could suck the bone marrow out of a dick.

"Look, I haven't chased anybody down. You got me confused with the next man."

"How can I confuse them scars on your face?" She snaked her neck and rolled her eyes in true ghetto girl fashion. "You running round this muthafucka looking like somebody played S.O.S on ya face. Ain't nobody in the world confusing that shit." When she poked her big lips poked out with that loud ass orange lipstick, Lincoln imagined jamming his whole dick down into her throat until she suffocated.

"Look, bitch, I told you it wasn't me now you better get the fuck on before I call my police friends down here to shut this whole lil' operation down for the weekend."

"Let's go!" the pimp stated quickly. He didn't

need anyone making his strip hot. The weekend was his big payday.

"But daddy!" she whined

"Bitch bring ya ass!" He snatched her by her hair forgetting she had on a wig. She stood there looking mortified while Lincoln and Mike broke into a fit of laughter. Under her wig were five braids going to the back that started at the middle of her head. The braids resembled tiny gray and black worms congregating on her head.

"You so damn embarrassing, bitch, you ain't got this shit attached?" the pimp yelled as he threw the wig at her in disgust. If it weren't for the fact that she was one of his best workers and the police presence, he would have kicked her ass right there on the corner.

"Fuck you, out here in these streets everything needs to be detachable," she shot back as she glared at Lincoln. She was about to get slick out the mouth but thought better of it. When he stopped laughing, he looked her directly in her eyes with a look that said she had fucked up. Mike didn't miss the exchange.

"Man what was that all about?" Mike asked once they were back in the car.

"Hell if I know, she might have just remembered me from being around here with you." Lincoln was at a loss for words. She had totally caught him off guard, but she would pay for that stunt she pulled and he had the perfect set up for her snitching ass.

Mike stared at Lincoln before pulling off. Something wasn't adding up but he would find out soon enough.

"You going to see the wife tonight?" Lincoln tried to change the subject. The air in the car was thick and made his lungs feel as if no oxygen was getting to them. He let the window down to let the night air blow on his face.

"I was thinking about it but I don't know if I can leave you alone. You out here kidnapping hoes and shit." Mike laughed but the look Lincoln shot him sent chills up and down his spine.

"Look, man, that's not funny. I told you and that Daffy Duck looking bitch it wasn't me. How you gon' believe a hoe wearing orange lipstick?" Lincoln broke his icy glare and smiled at Mike to let him know he was joking with him. Lincoln couldn't wait to get back there so he could bring the prostitute back to Zachariah so he could rip her apart. He wanted to use every last one of the toys on her.

"I'm just messing with you, man. The shit was just funny. Did you see those damn lips on her? Looked like she could suck the chrome off a tailpipe." They both broke out into a fit of laughter. Lincoln knew he couldn't have been the only one to notice those soup coolers. "But yeah the wife is in heat so I'm gon' stop by for a little bit." Mike didn't really want to leave Lincoln, but he didn't want to make it seem like he didn't trust him anymore. He would do his own private investigating. Mike prayed his friend was on the up and up.

Lincoln dropped Mike off at his home and started on his way back to the strip to take care of loose lips. If she talked to too many people, she could cause some problems. He felt his phone vibrating on his hip. He looked at the screen and smiled.

"Hey Ma, what's up?" he asked cheerfully as he pulled over on the side of road to give her his full attention.

"Just checking on my baby. When are you coming over to visit? I have seen you in years it feels like."

"Really Jill Reynolds?"

"Yes Lincoln Zachariah Donaldson! You saying my damn name don't make any difference boy." Jill always exaggerated how long it had been since she had seen him to make him feel guilty.

"I just saw you last week! But I digress, lady, we will be over this weekend I promise."

"We?"

"Yes, ma'am, me and Gabrielle will be over this weekend."

"Well hell, I got to get out my good china for this auspicious occasion!" She was almost yelling in his ear she was so excited.

"Calm down, Ma, we not getting married or nothing."

"Hey now don't be pissing in my damn corn flakes! I'm just happy my baby got somebody that he's willing to bring home to momma!"

"Now we need to get you somebody."

"Now don't go worrying about that foolishness, this old lady is just fine. I got a bag full of goodies under my pillow. They don't talk back and I ain't got to get up and fix 'em nothing to eat afterwards."

"See here you go. Don't make me come over there and do some spring-cleaning. I'll throw that whole lil' bag away."

"Let me explain something to you son. If you throw anything away out of my bag of goodness, you won't throw nothing else away I promise ya that!"

"I don't like you being alone in that house Ma."

"I been alone in this house for years, now if you want to send someone to me, tell that little boy Mike to come over and I'll teach him a few thangs," she laughed.

"Really, Ma? That man is married." Jill always had quick come back that made Lincoln laugh. As long as he had known her, she'd been a spunky little lady that was never able to filter her thoughts. She just said whatever came to her mind.

"That's fine with me. That just means I get to keep my bed to myself when he leaves," she chuckled.

"Bye, lady, I can't deal with you tonight." He laughed and cringed at the same time. He couldn't imagine her getting it on with anyone let alone his partner Mike.

"Ok, baby, I'll see you Sunday?" she asked.

"Yes ma'am."

"Ok love you."

"Love you too." Lincoln smiled as he hung up the phone. He couldn't imagine what his life would have been like had he been placed anywhere else. She was a godsend to him and he loved her dearly for everything she had done for him.

When Lincoln had first arrived at her house, he wouldn't talk or eat, but she never gave up on him. She was there when he woke up in the middle of the night screaming from his nightmares. It had gotten to the point where she slept in a Lazy Boy chair in his room just so he could feel safe. He thought about everything he had done in his life and knew it would break her heart to know what he and Zachariah had been up to all these years.

Instead of going back to the strip, he drove around aimlessly reminiscing on his childhood.

*****

"Miss Jill," Lincoln looked up at her with tears in his eyes.

"Yes, baby, what's wrong?" She noticed a worried look in his eyes. She had been sitting in his room with him ever since he had awakened from one of his nightmares.

Jill's heart broke over the pain she could clearly see in the young boy's eyes. She knew there was nothing she could do about the pain and torturous feelings that had taken up residence in his spirit.

"Why didn't she like me?" he cried.

"Honey I don't think it was that she didn't like you." She got up from her Lazy Boy chair, walked over to his bed, and sat down slowly. He still wasn't used to being with her. Lincoln had been with her for a little over a year with no real change, but she was going to be as patient as possible with him. She couldn't have kids, she'd had a full hysterectomy at the tender age of sixteen because of some girls at her school didn't like her and they jumped her causing too much damage to repair in her uterus. "Your mother was a sick lady." She reached out and rubbed his face. He flinched and she pulled her hand away quickly.

"How was she sick? Do I have it?" he questioned.

"I don't know, baby, but any person that would do that to a child has to be some kind of sick." Jill never understood how someone could hurt a child in such a way. She would sell her soul to the devil if he had promised her a child. She had always wanted a big family but knew it would never be naturally possible.

Jill went into nursing as a way to stay close to children and to help heal them. She had always questioned God on why he cursed her with a womb that didn't work. However, when she met Lincoln, it all came together and she stopped questioning God. She knew she was sent to save, love, and take care of Lincoln. Having Lincoln to love gave her back her faith in God. She had thought that God had given up on her and wasn't listening to her prayers.

"And no, I don't think you are sick. You are perfect sweetie." She reached for his hand and this time he didn't move.

"Well, why do I dream about her all the time? She always hurts me. I don't know what I did to her." He was crying but Jill could see a mixture of pain and anger in his eyes.

Jill looked him in the eyes and couldn't come up with an excuse because honestly there was no excuse for the abuse he had suffered.

"I can't answer that, honey. I'm afraid that's a question we will never know the answer to." She pulled him up into her arms to embrace him and held him tightly. "But I do know that I will never let anyone or anything ever hurt you again. I promise."

That night, a bond was made between the two of them that would be stronger than that of him and his biological mother.

*****

A horn blowing brought Lincoln back to the present. He hadn't even noticed he had been sitting at a stop sign for about fifteen minutes in a daze.

"You love her more than me, don't you?" Dorothy said more as an observation than a question.

"Who, Mother?" Lincoln huffed, not feeling her

presence at all. He knew Dorothy had been jealous of his and Jill's relationship. However, in his opinion, she had absolutely no room to feel any type of way about their relationship.

"Don't play dumb with me son. The one you call momma!"

"Well she has never tried to kill me so that's a plus on her part," he said sarcastically.

"I asked you a question."

"Yes, I love her more than you. She raised me, the right way, might I add."

"And you still turned out to be a murderer like I knew you would," she shot back.

"You knew I would because you made sure of it!" Lincoln banged his fist against the steering wheel.

"What I should have made sure of is that you never made it through the birth canal."

"Well you didn't and now I'm here and you are not!" Lincoln's heart was beating fast as he gripped the steering wheel trying to control his anger. She had hit a nerve, he knew she hated him, but she had never said anything like that to him. "Would you just go away?"

Knocking on his window almost made him jump out of his skin. He looked up to see he was in front of Mike's house and Mike was looking at him like he'd lost him mind. He reached up and hit the unlock button on the door.

"Aye you alright?" Mike had concern etched across his face. Lincoln took in slow breaths to steady his breathing. He could feel his anxiety attacks starting to come back. Sometimes they would get so severe that he would pass out. He needed to see Dr. Langston immediately.

"Nah I'm good, just going down memory lane a lil' bit." He shook his head.

"You sweating and shit, you need to go home?"

"Yeah I think I need to. I'm not feeling this tonight. I need to clear my mind." For some reason the conversation with his mother had really shaken him up. He didn't know if it was his mother's words alone or the hooker shooting off at the mouth earlier that had him on edge. Whatever the case, his nerves were shot.

"A'ight."

17
SEEKING EVIL

Mike was from what most people would call old money. His family had fled from Ireland during The Great Famine to St. Louis, MO in the late 1840s. The Famine was a potato disease known as potato blight, which ravaged potato crops throughout Europe. Almost one million people died during that time of starvation, disease, and emigration.

Mike's great-great-grandfather William packed up his family and ran to St. Louis for fear of getting sick and dying. With what little money he had, he got in on the fur trade. Since St. Louis sat in the most popular area of the Mississippi river trading post, he became a very wealthy man.

The men of the family didn't follow in William's footsteps though. They were all in some part of the military or policemen. So as a child Mike had always dreamed of being like the men in his family. Mike's honor code was strict and he hoped and prayed that he wouldn't have to turn his best friend in for murder. No matter how much he loved Lincoln, he would never be able to live with himself knowing he let his friend get away with being a murderer.

Once Mike dropped Lincoln off at the station, he headed for the strip where he and Lincoln patrolled at night. He couldn't stop thinking about what the loudmouth hooker had said about Lincoln earlier that evening. He always wondered what Lincoln did after he dropped him off to his wife; but being a killer never once crossed his mind.

Lincoln had been through a lot in his young twenty-five years. Mike didn't know how Lincoln was able to come out of his childhood with his sanity intact.

He pulled up and looked around for the pimp and hooker from earlier but didn't see them anywhere. He looked down at his watch; it was 3:24 am. He had four hours left on his shift and planned make good use of it.

Mike got out of his car and walked up to a couple of prostitutes standing on the corner. He let his eyes roam their frames. One of the ladies was wearing a purple wig that hung down her back. She was dressed in a lime green cat suit with the sides cut out. The stitching in the material was being stretched to its capacity by the blubber that filled her stomach and ass. Although cute in the face, you could tell she had been on the streets for most of her life. The other lady wasn't as extravagant as her counterpart was. She was dress in a black mini skirt and Tupac Shakur tank top and some fishnet stockings. Mike was almost sure the crotch was cut out. The bags under her eyes could hold a roll of ten dollars' worth of quarters.

"Hello, ladies, can I talk to you for a minute?" He smiled at them because it looked like they were about to break into a sprint.

"We ain't doing nothing Officer, we just chilling," the one in the cat suit stated as she plastered on a fake smile practically showing all thirty-two teeth in her mouth.

"I'm not here to bother you. I just want to know if you've seen anyone that looks suspicious hanging around."

"Is that some sort of a joke pig?" Cat suit looked him up and down. "Every muthafucka around here looks suspicious. Look over there, that crack head about to snatch that woman's purse," cat suit lady said as pointed to a shifty looking character standing across the street from where they were standing. "That fool over there looking on the ground for imaginary crack is about to snap and kill everybody out here once he figure out ain't no more crack," she said seriously. "And…"

"Ok I get it." He didn't want her to go down the whole line of crack head adventures going on. "What are your names?"

"TaQuanda and this is Destiny," cat suite spoke again.

"Ok, TaQuanda, did you know that the prostitutes around here are coming up missing? Have you noticed anything out the ordinary?" He was losing his patience with the loud mouth woman.

"You know for you to be such a handsome white boy, you sure do ask some of the dumbest questions," TaQuanda spoke.

"Yeah we heard something about that. Are we in danger?" Destiny asked speaking for the first time. Sometimes she couldn't stand TaQuanda. In her opinion she talked entirely too much. TaQuanda was Destiny's back up though and no one dared to mess with her while she was with her.

"I can't say for sure. We are investigating it though. You might want to get off the streets until he is caught though." Mike turned his attention to Destiny; she seemed to be the one with some sense out of the duo.

"You muthafuckas don't give two shits about us bottom feeders," TaQuanda snorted. "Hoes been dying out this bitch for years and ain't nan one of you cock suckers ever came down to see about us! I bet some lil' white bitch done disappeared and now y'all out in full force, fuck outta here." She waved her hand at him.

"Look, ma'am, we can't do our jobs if we don't have any help. How are we supposed to know if something is wrong if everyone is so tight-lipped around this muthafucka? Everybody wants help but don't want to give any. So you can save that shit for the next pig." He could tell his language had caught them off guard but if she wanted to get indignant so could he. "Now I'm out here trying to find out what's happening to your hoe clique and you still don't want to help, fine," he huffed as he turned to walk away, thinking about another way to get info out of these people.

"Well damn you ain't have to say it like that, nigga," TaQuanda addressed Mike. He was used to being called a nigga. Black folks didn't discriminate on who they called a nigga. "I haven't seen anyone that looks out of place."

Mike seemed genuine and made TaQuanda want to help him out. She wanted him to find the killer. Her sister Daija had disappeared. She hadn't seen nor heard from her sister in a couple of weeks. It was normal for them to go at the most a week but she still hadn't heard from her. She prayed the man Mike was talking about didn't have her sister. "You got a card?" She rolled her eyes, he may have seemed genuine, but police were still the enemy.

Mike stopped in his tracks and reached in his pocket to retrieve one of his cards to give to her.

"Thank you," he said as he handed her the card.

"No need for all that. Gotta look out for my peoples." She shrugged as she studied the card's contents. She let his name Officer Mike Owens roll around in her head a few times then stepped back.

"Ok, again thank you ladies and be careful out here. Call me if you need me." He got in the car and drove off; he had a lot to think about.

*****

Lincoln watched from a distance as Mike interacted with a couple of prostitutes. He wondered what they had told him. He prayed he wouldn't have to kill his best friend. He and Mike had become very close but he would end him if he tried to take matters into his own hands.

He looked around for the pimp and the lady with the big lips covered in orange lipstick, but he didn't see them anywhere in sight. He knew for sure he had to get her off the streets. Things were getting hot around his stomping grounds, but he had never had any problems with venturing out to find new whores for Zachariah to kill.

Lincoln felt like his life was one big contradiction. While he knew that killing was wrong he still led the prostitutes to the slaughterhouse like a herd of sheep. He and Zachariah were supposed to be the will of the Lord but he was also sinning by murdering the women.

Exodus 20:13 states that thou shalt not kill, but what if it was in the name of the Lord? How was he judging these people when he himself was just as horrible if not worse than they were?

Lincoln wondered if his mother was there when Zachariah had sex with those women. Was she there when he had sex with Gabrielle? Would she let him keep her or would she try to come between them like she had done with him and Monique? He would never hurt Gabrielle though; he would end everything around him before he would hurt her.

He picked up his phone and stared at Gabrielle's name but scrolled pass it. He didn't know why but for as much as his heart longed for Gabrielle, something was telling to stay away from her. He went to Dr. Langston's number and pressed the call button. He hoped she answered because he really needed to talk to someone.

After a few rings, she answered.

"Hello?" She sounded groggy.

"Dr. Langston?"

"Yes Lincoln what's going on?" She turned to look at the clock to see what time it was. It was four o'clock in the morning.

"I'm in a lot of trouble."

"What kind of trouble?" She sat up in bed.

"Can I see you? I need to talk to someone about what I've been doing." He could feel the tears trying to fall from his eyes but he shook them off. "And I'm afraid of what I may do next."

"Yes come on in. I'll meet you there."

*****

Dr. Langston sat on the side of her bed for a minute thinking about Lincoln. When he was younger, she couldn't get him to open up to her for nothing in the world. He was a psychiatrist's dream case, everything he had been through she could surely get a good book out of him. She was forty years old, had been a psychiatrist for 14 years, and

Lincoln had been her dream case when he came along. She had mostly been dealing with people with severe depression, bulimia, and suicidal thoughts.

Dr. Langston could still remember when she'd first started out as a psychiatrist. Ninety percent of the cases she had thrown at her left her sitting flabbergasted. During one of her first sessions, there was a seventeen-year-old boy who suffered from Corophagi. The conversation was still fresh in her head as if it happened yesterday.

"So what brings you and your family in to see me Christopher?" Dr. Langston addressed the teenager. He sat with his head hung low. His long greasy locks of hair hung wildly all over his head and cascaded down over his face. He wore all black and she could smell his body odor from where she sat.

"Well Dr. Langston it seems that Christopher likes to eat shit!" the boy's mother stated in a matter of fact tone.

"Excuse me?" Dr. Langston sat up straight in her chair. She couldn't have heard her correctly. She looked from the mother to boy to try and get a good look at his face, but his hair covered his whole face.

"Exactly what I said! He likes to partake in shitty cuisine. Dog shit, cat shit, bird shit, my shit, his shit, your shit, everybody's shit!"

It took everything in within Dr. Langston's soul not burst into a fit of laughter. The mother looked like June Cleaver and looked like she had never said

a curse word a day in her life. The dad sat silent
with his face beet red from embarrassment. Dr.
Langston couldn't decipher whether he was more
embarrassed by his wife or son.

"Hm," Dr. Langston cleared her throat. "Well
when did all of this start Christopher?" She looked
to the boy.

"Does is really matter when it started lady?" Just
give him something to make it stop!" Dr. Langston
totally understood where the mother was coming
from, because who wants to know their child is
eating bowel movements.

"Well, yes, it does matter. I need to know what
brought this about," Dr. Langston addressed the
mother then turned her attention back to
Christopher. "Now can you tell me when it started
Christopher?" Silence, he only shrugged his
shoulders.

"See this is the shit we have to deal with! Pun
intended! I thought if Bill kicked his ass, he would
stop, but that didn't help at all. Do you got any
drugs Doc?"

The cold chill of the air conditioner kicking on
brought her out of memory lane. That had been
close to fifteen years ago and even though she
remembered it like it was yesterday, no one topped
Lincoln for her. He seemed to be suffering from a
multitude of mental disorders, cyclomythia (a form
of severe depression), hallucinations, Dissociative
Identity Disorder, and Schizophrenia. She knew it
would take a while to decipher which one he had. If

only Lincoln would let her in more, she would be able to help him and get him on the right regimen and headed to some sort of peace.

When he stopped coming to her, she never forgot about him, often thought of him, and often wondered what ever became of him. She got up and got dressed. She looked at herself in the mirror and admired her beauty. She wore her hair in a tight ponytail to the back that showed off her high cheekbones and thick eyebrows. She had never been married or had any kids. The men in her life couldn't handle her work schedule. It didn't matter what time of night it was, if one of her patients needed her, she would be there to talk them off whatever ledge they were on.

18
MEETING EVIL

Dr. Langston watched Lincoln intently as he paced back and forth in front of her. She regarded how he fidgeted and tapped his fingers against his thighs as if he was playing the piano or counting something. She silently took notes because she didn't want to disturb him. His back was hunched and his head hung low. Frustration was etched across his forehead. Lincoln held a conversation with himself as if he was trying to get his thoughts in order before he addressed her.

"Doc I don't know what I'm doing anymore," Lincoln huffed as he stopped and looked Dr. Langston in the eyes. He was on the verge of tears and what looked to be a serious nervous breakdown.

"Can you elaborate on that for me?" Dr. Langston prayed he was about to get the breakthrough she had been waiting on for the last 10 plus years.

"Can I start out with the nightmares I've been having?" The question caught Dr. Langston off guard because it sounded like a little kid asking if he could stay up a little longer to watch television.

"Yes, Lincoln, start wherever you feel the need."

Lincoln stopped pacing and sat down on the tan leather couch right across from Dr. Langston. He thought for a minute about what he was about to do. How would she react to his living nightmare? How would she look at him after she found out the things that went on his head? He knew honestly, there was no one in the world who would understand his situation.

"My nightmares always start out about my mother." He closed his eyes tightly at the thoughts of his mother.

"What is your mother doing in these dreams Lincoln?"

"She is beating me while I recite scriptures from the Bible." She could see his fist clench shut and the muscles in his jaw tighten.

"Why is she beating you?"

"Because I asked for food." His voice cracked and Dr. Langston's heart sank a little at the revelation.

"I asked her if there was anything to eat. Not realizing she was still going through one of her mental breakdowns. I was young then I didn't know what was going on with her. All I knew is that I had to get through her to get to some food. I hadn't eaten in three days. She'd had me locked in my room for those three days. That evening I went to test the doorknob to see if it was unlocked and it was." Lincoln paused for a minute to collect himself. He had never really talked to anyone about his nightmare in such depth before.

"You see, Doc, my dreams were my actual reality. What you would call a nightmare was just another day in my childhood."

"I see," was all Dr. Langston could get out. She just wanted him to get on with the story, never had she been as engrossed in someone's life as she was with Lincoln.

"I walked into the living room while she was kneeling down in front of her Jesus statue. I watched her rock back and forth, as she recited the same scripture over and over again. Ye though I walk through the valley of shadow of death, I will fear no evil; for thou art with me; thy rod and shaft they comfort me. My mother could recite the whole Bible to you." He paused again preparing himself to say out loud what he had been holding in for years.

"I interrupted her prayer. I was eight, in a lot of pain and starving. So I figured her prayer could be paused," he said with a shrug of his shoulders. "Momma, I called to her, but she just kept on praying and rocking back and forth. So I walked up to her and touched her shoulder. Before I knew what was happening, she had pulled me down to the floor and smashed my head in the feet of the Jesus statue." He took a deep breath. "Blood oozed from the gash that had opened up on my forehead."

"Repent, she said to me, but I couldn't talk. My head was spinning and I had blood running into my eyes. Repent, she yelled again while holding the back of my head. But I didn't want to pray, I wanted to eat, no, I needed to eat. But she was so far gone she couldn't see me as her starving child, she only saw a sinner there with her." He shook his head.

"Would you like to take a break?" Dr. Langston asked interrupting him. She could see this was starting to get to him by the way his body would tense up every so often. He had begun digging his nails into the skin of his forearms.

"No, Doc, I need to get this out. There is no telling when I will be willing to tell this story again."

"Ok continue then, Lincoln." During any other session, she would have stopped her patient because she wouldn't want them to get too worked up and go into a shell or even worse a psychotic break where they could hurt themselves or her.

"Only sinners and evil doers refuse to repent to the Lord. Which one are you. Her voice was cold, almost robotic. I told her I was neither once I found my voice. My head hurt so much I was seeing stars. She was squeezing my neck so hard I knew my spine would snap at any moment. Are you ready to pray, she asked me. I nodded my head, yes, as best I could, but I wasn't. I was so hungry I thought I was gonna pass out if I didn't get something to eat soon." Unconsciously he rubbed his stomach as if he was feeling those hunger pains again.

"Repent ye, therefore, and be converted, that your sins may be blotted out. Momma, I'm hungry, I stopped the prayer again. Before I could duck, she had grabbed me by my neck and thrown me across the room. She was rushing towards me as I scrambled to my feet to run away but she was lightning fast when she was in the zone; she had super human powers. She grabbed me by the face and tossed my like a rag doll back over in front the Jesus statue. Pray sinner, she yelled as she smashed my face into Jesus' feet again, but I didn't have to the strength to pray. I didn't want to pray to a God who would allow this to happen to me. Why would he let her continue to abuse me that way? I hadn't done nothing wrong to anyone. I figured I must had been a real bad person in my past lives. When I didn't pray she rammed my head into his feet over and over again until she eventually knocked me out." He sat up and looked Dr. Langston in her eyes. He was searching for some sort of reaction but there was none.

"So is this the same dream you have every night?" She held her poker face, but on the inside, she was hurting. She wanted to cry for him, but she held on to her professional face.

"Most of the time, yeah, but there are more. I won't put too much on you at one time," he chuckled.

"It would be no problem for me. Remember, I'm here for you whenever you need me." And she meant that. She was so engrossed in getting his story she hadn't even been charging him.

"Thank you, Doc, for letting me vent to you. I'll be back soon." He stood to leave and she followed. His story had drained her too.

"I look forward to seeing you again soon, just call when you're ready." As they reached the door to her office, Lincoln turned to her and just stared for a minute before he finally spoke.

"Are you entertained yet? If not just hold on it's going to get real interesting, sinner." Then he turned and walked away.

Dr. Langston stood there stunned, because it wasn't Lincoln or Zachariah's voice. This voice had a feminine pitch to it, which let her know that it was his mother speaking right then. She wished she could call in one of her colleagues to help with the case, but she knew Lincoln would totally shut down in the company of someone new. She wanted to hold on a diagnosis at that point. She wasn't sold on him having that many disorders just yet, but she would get to the bottom of everything if he allowed it.

19
THE REAPING

"Ma!" Lincoln yelled as he walked into his mother's home. He looked around and didn't see her anywhere but he knew she was there because of the aroma of good cooking lingering in the air.

"Maybe she'll answer me," Mike boasted as he walked up behind Lincoln. "You know she loves me right?"

"Yeah make me call Michelle and tell her where your ass is at."

"Is that my baby?" Jill squealed as she rounded the corner wiping her hands on her sexiest cook apron.

"Yes," Lincoln and Mike said in unison.

"Well aren't you a beautiful little thing!" Jill walked right up Gabrielle. When she walked in and saw Gabrielle, tunnel vision kicked in, and all she saw was the woman in Lincoln's life.

"Thank you; I'm Gabrielle, nice to meet you."
Gabrielle blushed as she stuck out her hand for a
handshake.

"Girl you better put that hand away and give me
a hug." Jill pulled her in for a tight squeeze. She
was so excited Lincoln had finally brought someone
home she didn't know what to do with herself.

"Hm," Mike cleared his throat.

"Oh, sweetheart, I was making my way to you."
Jill smiled at him. "Your wife ain't here is she? I
don't want her trying to fight me for holding on too
long," she joked as she embraced him.

"She's at home so you hold on as long as you
want," Mike said as looked at Lincoln and smiled
mischievously at him.

"See this the mess I have to deal with when I
bring them two around each other. Are you gon'
have any hugs left for me Momma?" Lincoln held
his arms out.

"You know I got all the hugs in the world for
you sweetheart. But I hear my green beans boiling
over." She let go of Mike and walked swiftly to the
kitchen.

"It sure smells good in here Ms. Jill," Gabrielle
said as the aroma invaded her senses. Her stomach
started growling the moment she walked into the
house. She looked around the home; it had a
comfortable grandma's house feel to it. The walls
and mantel was covered in pictures of Jill and
Lincoln. It was like they were all each other had.

There was one picture of Mike and his family but that was the only one that didn't contain a picture of Lincoln.

"Quit it with that Ms. Jill mess. The folks round here call me Momma!" Jill yelled from the kitchen. "Now y'all go on and sit at the table, I'll bring the food in a minute."

Gabrielle watched as Lincoln interacted with Jill. She loved seeing him smiling and laughing. She had seen him smile before but it was something different when he was with his adopted mother. She could tell Jill meant a lot to him the way he catered to her. She wanted to be able to make him smile like that. Jealousy tried to rear its ugly head but she shook those thoughts quickly. A man and his mother have an unspoken bond and love that no one would ever be able to understand nor penetrate. No, she would get in where she fit in.

"Excuse me; I have to go to the bathroom. Not that anyone would notice with you two making googly eyes at each other the whole time. Both y'all gon' make me shoot something," Lincoln joked as he went to the bathroom.

"Boy hush up and stop hating!" Everyone laughed at Jill's attempt at sounding hip.

On his way back, he stopped by the living room and noticed that there was breaking news on Fox 2. He walked in closer and turned up the volume. There was a house that been set on fire.

"I am Dian Leaks and I'm reporting live from where a house was allegedly set on fire intentionally while a mother and her daughter slept. The bodies of 49-year-old Dana Johnson and 31-year-old Vonna Johnson were found around 3:30 this morning. According to witnesses, the girlfriend of the victim's brother was seen throwing something into the home and short while later the house caught fire."

"Damn where was this at?" Mike walked up to him and asked.

"Somewhere in Norwoods," Lincoln answered as a picture of the suspect was shown on the screen. He felt every muscle in his body tense up. Her beady eyes stared at him taunting him. From the mug shot, he could tell that life had dealt her a shitty hand. Her facial features looked rough and her hair was cut off but looked like it needed a shape up and some shampoo.

Lincoln's body had gone warm all over and there was a tingly feeling floating up and down his spine. He prayed no one would turn her in so he could find her first and make her pay for this. Visions of his torture session ran through his head and felt tingly at the vision playing in his head. Lincoln didn't know if he would be letting Zachariah take part in this party. From what he had heard, the woman and her daughter had nothing to do with the domestic issues the lady had with the victim's brother, but the mother and daughter had paid for his shenanigans. The story tugged at his heartstrings. Another senseless death. An innocent mother and her child gone from the world for something they had nothing to do with.

"You alright baby?" Gabrielle could feel that his mood had changed.

"I'm good, let's finish eating." He took one last look at the screen then went to finish the night. He didn't want to ruin everyone's nice time because he had gotten in his feelings about someone he hadn't even met before.

*****

It didn't take long for Lincoln to find the accused murderer. He had gone to the police station and gathered up as much info about her as possible. Her name was Seresa Graham and she might be hiding out at her mother's home. When he went to the house, she wasn't there, so he sat outside her mother's home and followed her mother around until she led him to Seresa.

The mother had left the house with two suitcases and looked like she was in a rush. It was 1:30 in the morning so he figured she was trying to sneak her daughter out of town. He wanted to choke the life out of the mother for trying to help the killer. How could she help a murderer? He wondered if either of his mothers ever loved him enough to help him get away with a crime so heinous.

Lincoln followed her to an apartment complex. She got out and took the suitcases into an apartment and left. He'd hoped Seresa would have come out too, but she didn't so he would have to play the waiting game. He didn't have to wait too long. About an hour later, she came out looking around like a paranoid crack head. He followed her long enough till she was alone on a road far out and pulled out the cherry light that he had taken from the police station for situations such as this one, when he wasn't in his police car.

Lincoln turned on the lights. He could see Seresa's neck stretch up to the rearview mirror to see exactly where the light was coming from. He thought she was about to take off and was preparing to give chase, but she slowed down and stopped on the side of the highway. The highway was practically deserted but he knew he needed to move fast. There is always someone watching even when you don't think there is.

He got out and walked to the driver's side of the car.

"License and registration ma'am," he spoke without even looking at her. He was too busy watching the highway; hoping another cop car didn't pull up trying to help him out.

"Can you tell me what I did Officer?" Seresa looked up but couldn't see his face. He had a bright flashlight shining down into her eyes.

"For starters," he began as he pulled out his stun gun, "you're a piece of shit scumbag that needs to be brought to justice." Right then, Lincoln could see a light go off in her head, recognition that she was in trouble and had been caught. She went to put her foot on the gas pedal but the car was in park. Lincoln aimed the stun gun and the wires latched onto the skin of her neck. He watched as her teeth clenched shut and her eyes rolled to the back of her head as her body went rigid and shook violently right before she passed out.

When Seresa woke up all four of her limbs were strapped to a wooden table type of contraption. The Rack had become one of Lincoln's favorite toys after watching what it had done to the prostitute, but she wouldn't get the luxury of dying so quickly, no she would suffer a long and torturous death. Lincoln had brought the wrath God on plenty of sinners but she would be one that he would surely enjoy.

Seresa watched as he set out different things she guessed he planned to use on her, some she had never seen before and the ones she did recognize, she prayed he wasn't going to use on her. She recognized a jar of honey and jar of fire red ants that sat on the table with her. There was a small but long rake looking thing lying next to her also.

Seresa was so caught up in what was laying on the table next to her that the flicking of the switch on the blowtorch that Lincoln had been playing with scared her so badly she pissed on herself. Lincoln turned to her at the sound of the fluids running on to the floor. He looked like a worker from the CDC. He had on a full body hazmat suit with thick rubber gloves and goggles that covered half his face.

Lincoln was being extra careful when it came to those fire ants. He wasn't taking any chance of them getting on his skin. He knew they made an ugly mess out of flesh and he wanted no parts of that.

"What is all this about?" Seresa finally found her

voice.

"It's about the wrath of the Lord being brought upon you for your treacherous sins."

"Please, man, you don't have to do this; I was going to turn myself in," she cried. She had no idea that someone had witnessed her crimes, but when she started getting phone calls about her being on the news she knew she had fucked up. She had enlisted the help of her mother to help her get out of town.

"Oh really, when? When you came back from your mini-vacation in California?" A shocked look spread across her face.

"Seresa is it? Did I pronounce it right?" She nodded her head giving conformation that he had indeed pronounce it correctly. "It's people like you who make this world the horrible place it is. We are in the end of times and with the stunt you pulled what side of the gate do you think you will be on?" He paused from gathering his utensils to look at her. "But I'll let you explain yourself to God when you get to the gates. As for now, the grim reaper is here and your words mean nothing, so let's skip the pleasantries, it's time to get this party started."

"Please don't do this," she begged.

"Don't you think that's what the lady and her daughter would have said if they knew you would be taking their lives that night? Did you wait around to listen to their screams? Did you even care that you were about to set two innocent people on fire?" He felt his body go warm and his face went numb at the thought of those two ladies being set on fire.

"Please...I didn't mean..." she stopped talking when he fired up the blowtorch again.

"Behold, he cometh with clouds; and every eye shall see him, they which pierced him, and all kindreds of the earth shall wail because of him," Lincoln said as placed the ball with the strap attached to it in her mouth. He snapped it snuggly around her head so it wouldn't come off.

She shook her head at a rapid speed trying to speak to him; he could hear her muffled screams but paid them no mind. Lincoln reached over and picked up the blowtorch.

"I'm going to show you very slowly how it feels to be set on fire." Her body bucked wildly trying to get away from Lincoln and the hot flames he had coming out of the blowtorch. He placed the flame from the blowtorch against her nipple and watched as blisters formed instantly on her breast. The skin melted away leaving a gaping hole where her nipple used to be. The screams that came from her were like nothing he had ever heard.

"It doesn't feel so good does it? Did that man even do anything that bad to make you want kill to his family?" he asked as he put the torch on her breast again. The sizzling of her skin was making his skin crawl and his stomach flip but it was her Karma. She had to know what she had put those ladies though. The smell of burnt skin was somewhere between a rotting corpse and the back of a dump truck. He was about to blowtorch her whole body but then he remembered he had the Cat's Paw also known as the Spanish Tickler sitting there. It resembled a small rake, with an arm's length handle and the ends were razor sharp in the shape of claw.

When Lincoln read about the old Spanish torture device he knew that he needed one and couldn't wait to use it. He picked it up and stood at the top of the table looking down into her face. Her light brown skin turned ten different shades of red and her face had tears rolling down it. Her lips trembled with fear as her eyes begged for him to stop, but he couldn't stop, her lesson was far from over.

Lincoln placed the claw at the top of her foot and dragged it up her body, basically raking the flesh and meat from her bones. He pulled the Cat's Paw until he reached the top of her chest. He repeated this until the front of her body looked as if it had shredded. She had long ago passed out from the pain, but he had so much in store for her. He poured salt in the wounds on her chest to wake her back up. She woke up with a blood-curdling scream that Lincoln clearly heard even with the ball in her mouth. Lincoln was sure someone must have heard the screams. At that point, he was too far gone to care anymore.

"People who conceal their sins will not prosper, but if they confess and turn from them, they will receive mercy." Lincoln looked Seresa in the eyes as he took the ball from her mouth. "Are you ready to confess your sins sinner?"

She couldn't talk; the pain she was feeling too unbearable, so her response was the sound of her crying.

"You know you are the worse kind of sinner there is. You believe you did the right thing don't you?" he asked as he picked up the jar of ants and opened it. A few ants escaped as he taped a funnel to the top of the jar. He let them fall onto her open flesh and immediately they began feasting. Her cries got loud again.

"Oh God please! Oh God, please help me!" she screamed.

"Then I will return to my place until they admit their guilt and turn to me. For as soon as trouble comes, they will earnestly search for me."

"Please, I'm sorry; I didn't mean to do that. I didn't know her daughter was there!" she cried as she tried to explain her heinous decision.

"You are a drunk with no job and a shit load of kids that you do not take care of. You are lousy mother, the most precious gift a woman could ever receive, and you just left them for someone else to raise." During his short investigation, he had found out that she had plenty of kids spread throughout St. Louis and she was raising none of them. "And you expect a man to make you his wife? So when he decided you had to go, you decided to hurt him in the worst way possible." She began crying even louder.

Truth was at the moment Seresa set the house on fire she just wanted to hurt her ex-boyfriend. She knew he cherished his family and that he would lose his mind if anything happened to any of them, so since she couldn't have his heart, no one would. However, her actions had backfired on her. His sister had been nothing but nice to her and she lost her life in return. Now she was about to lose her life as well.

"Women kill me thinking that their pussy will save them. You do know that for every one man there are ten women right?" He placed his gloved finger over the hole at the top of the funnel and began to shake the ants up to get them in an uproar. He used his free hand to open the jar of honey. He stuck his fingers into the jar, pulled it out covered in the honey, and then pushed them into her vagina, as far they would go. He wanted to make sure he set all of her insides on fire. "So in your next life remember you need to bring something more to the table than just smelly pussy."

"Please don't do this; I said I was sorry!"

"Does it look like a give a fuck about your punk ass sorry?" he yelled as he gripped her face. "That sorry don't mean shit! You're only sorry you got caught! I'm tired your existence."

"He shoved the funnel as far as it would go and began to tap the end of the jar so the ants would fall on or crawl into her vagina. Once he was satisfied with the amount that had fallen in, he pulled the jar away and stepped back to watch her squirm. He guessed they had begun to feast because her body began to shake as she raised up off the table repeatedly. She screamed at the top of her lungs as they ate at her insides.

The ants began to file out onto her body. He tried to pour some ants onto her eyes but he was so nervous with ants all around that he spilled the whole jar on the table. He jumped back and onto a table that was nearby. He watched in horror as the ants covered her body like a blanket. She screamed until the ants went into her mouth and shut her up for good. He was pissed; he had wanted to use the ants on different parts of her body for hours. He sat down on the table for what felt like hours and watched as her flesh turned into bone. Once he couldn't stomach it any more, he set the table on fire and watched the ants die and her bones turn to ash.

As he was cleaning up her remains, he vowed she would be his last kill for the Lord.

20
LET ME LIVE

Gabrielle was giddy with excitement that Lincoln had called and said he wanted to go out to eat. Yes, they spent time together, but they had yet to hold a long meaningful conversation because Lincoln was always running away, and he had been so sporadic with his visits and when she would see him. She felt in her gut that he would never do anything to hurt her, but she had been hurt so much in her life that she couldn't help but to feel some kind of way.

"What's going on in that head of yours lil' lady?" Lincoln asked Gabrielle because she had gotten very quiet at the dinner table. A plethora of emotions flashed across her face as if she was in deep thought.

"Huh? Oh no I'm good, did you say something?" She didn't want to ruffle his feathers by bringing up his disappearing acts. No, she would take him, however she could get him.

"You sure? It looks like you were thinking something serious." He could feel that something was bothering her.

"Oh no I'm fine." She waved him off. "Just thinking about my life and where I thought I would be by now."

"So are you not where you want to be in life?" She had peeked Lincoln's curiosity.

"No not at all, I mean I know every woman longs to be able to be just a housewife and not have to do anything but be a good wife, but it was hell for me even before the abuse started. I never knew he didn't want me to work." She shrugged her shoulders. "Guess that's what I get for leaping before thinking."

"What happened was not your fault."

"Yeah it was. But I've always wanted to be a world famous archeologist that travels the world looking for ancient artifacts and bones." Lincoln loved the way her eyes lit up when she talked about her dreams. Her smile was bright and her eyes sparkled.

"What is the one place you would go if given the chance?"

"Oh my ultimate dream trip would be to Jerusalem. I want to go to the holiest place in the world." When she said that, Lincoln felt something stir inside him. "I want to visit where Jesus spent his last days, where the last supper took place. I want to feel the atmosphere of where the crucifixion and the resurrection took place."

"What draws you to this place?" Lincoln was intrigued by her revelation.

"I've always been interested in ancient history of any kind; and Jerusalem is rich with ancient history. The city of peace. I just want to feel the air on my skin, feel the air in my lungs, and feel the energy in my veins. Can you imagine what the aura of that place feels like?" His excitement escalated again.

"I've never thought about that way."

"Is it crazy that I want to visit the sacred tomb of Mary while drinking a glass of Henri Jayer Riche Bourge wine?" She chuckled. "It's a rare wine that was only made in Jerusalem but it's not made anymore."

"No it's not crazy. Though I've never thought to bring wine into such a holy place. But if Jesus can turn water into wine it can't be that bad right?" He joined in on the laughter.

Gabrielle couldn't contain her excitement. They had finally gotten a chance to talk and laugh. Everything had always been so tense with them.

"I had such a good time tonight Lincoln," Gabrielle said as they walked into her hotel room.

"It was my pleasure and thank you for teaching me about Jerusalem. I really enjoyed it." He watched her blush like a little schoolgirl.

"Thank you," she smiled and put her head down.

She had thought she had bored him to death the whole night.

"Stop putting your head down. You are beautiful, intelligent, and the most amazing woman I have ever met." He put his fingers under her chin to pull it back up so they were eye to eye. "I want you to be proud of you okay?" He could see the uncertainty in her eyes. He smiled at her because he knew it would wipe away any doubt in her heart.

Gabrielle could see the love in his eyes. His eyes were saying much more than his mouth had ever said.

"Can you make me feel what your eyes are saying?" she asked as she held his gaze. She wanted to feel the love in his eyes spill out all over her body.

"Say no more." Lincoln pulled his shirt over his head then slipped her dress down off her shoulders. She wore nothing under her dress, letting him know she had been ready all night. He placed his lips on hers as he guided her body back to the bed. "Lay down," he said in a demanding tone, and she did as she was told.

"Let me see you play with that pussy." He licked his lips with anticipation. She smiled mischievously as she opened her legs wide and slid two of her fingers inside of her pussy. She pulled them out and began rubbing her juices all over her clitoris.

"Can I taste it?" Lincoln asked as he crawled onto the bed with her.

"Uummmm hmmmm," she moaned as she stuck her fingers out for him to suck her essence off them. "Make love to me Lincoln, please?" she begged. Her body felt like it was on fire she was so hot and turned on. Lincoln did what was asked of him all night long taking both of them on an emotional high that neither of them wanted to come to down from. They made love until both of them passed out from exhaustion.

*****

"You know, Lincoln, one day you will become a sinner and then you will have to make the choice to repent and pray for forgiveness," Dorothy said to Lincoln while they sat at the dinner table.

"What's a sinner mother?" he asked just as innocently as six year old could have.

"A sinner is someone who doesn't live by the way of the Lord son."

"Are you a sinner? I want to be whatever you are Mother." He smiled at her not knowing the magnitude of the conversation.

"You little bastard your sinning ways are already showing!" She yanked him from the dinner table, dragged him into the living room, and dropped him in front of the Jesus statue.

"What did I do Mother?" He had no clue how he had went from talking to her now throwing him around.

"For God commanded, saying Honour thy father and mother and He that curseth father or mother, let him die the death" She rocked back and forth on her knees as she said this prayer over and over again. Lincoln jumped to his feet, took off running towards his room, and made it just in time to slam the door in her face and jump into his hiding spot.

"Lincoln!" Dorothy yelled at the top of her lungs. "Lincoln get your ass out here and repent before God punishes you!" Lincoln could hear the old floorboards creaking above him. He prayed she wouldn't find his hiding spot and that she would leave his room soon, but he had no such luck. She sat down in the middle of his bedroom on the floor and began screaming his name and praying to the Lord to forgive him for being disobedient.

"Forgive him oh Lord for he knows not what he is doing. Lincoln! Lincoln!"

*****

"Lincoln, Lincoln baby, wake up!" Gabrielle shook Lincoln to wake him from the nightmare he was having. He was shaking as if he had a fever and sweating like he was in a sauna. He wasn't fighting in his sleep, he just seemed like he was scared to death at whatever was happening to him.

Lincoln jumped out of the bed like it was on fire. He looked around as if he didn't have clue as to where he was. He took deep breaths in and out but it wasn't helping to calm him down. His fists were balled up as if he was ready to start swinging on anything breathing.

"Baby it's ok, you were having a nightmare," Gabrielle tried to assure him he was safe. He stood next to bed looking like a scared child. His chest heaved in and out as if he was having a hard time breathing. She went to get out of bed to help him but he moved away from her.

"Don't," was all he said as he went into the bathroom to throw some water on his face. He looked at himself in the mirror and shook his head at the person who was staring back him. He was becoming a shell of himself. His eyes were starting to sink and he was losing weight; the stress was getting to him. He knew if he didn't get some help soon he was going to disappear altogether.

He walked out of the bathroom and Gabrielle was sitting on the edge of the bed with tears in her eyes. He sat down and picked up his clothes. He couldn't even face her because he knew that she would want to talk about what was going on and she was last person that he wanted to talk about his situation with.

He dialed Dr. Langston's number and she picked up on the third ring.

"Hello Lincoln is everything ok?" she asked half asleep.

"I need to see you."

"Ok be there in twenty minutes."

"I have to go," Lincoln said as he put his clothes back on.

"Where are you going and who was that?" she asked scared to hear the answer.

"Someone who is helping me."

"Why can't I help you?"

"Because I didn't ask for your help. I'll be back in a lil' bit." He didn't mean to come off so harsh but he had no time to tend to her hurt feelings.

"But Lincoln…"

"Stop it, I'll see you later." He walked out slamming the door.

Gabrielle sat dumbfounded. She couldn't believe he had just ran out on her again. She thought they had gotten somewhere but she felt like they had just gone back to square one. Her heart was aching and longing for a love she felt she would never have. She grabbed her phone and turned on her Pandora. When found the Marsha Ambrosia station they were playing the perfect song. Melanie Fiona's "Wrong Side of the Love Song."

The last thing Gabrielle heard before she drifted off was Melanie crooning, "And I don't wanna be without you. 'Cause I can hardly breathe without you. This is what it feels like to be the one standing left behind. How did I become the wrong side of the love song?"

*****

"Doc she wasn't always a bad person," Lincoln explained to Dr. Langston.

"So what do you think happened?" Dr. Langston

sat across from Lincoln with her pen and pad in hand hoping this was the breakthrough she had been waiting on.

"When I got older I researched her symptoms and I think she had schizophrenia."

"And how did you come up with that conclusion?" Dr. Langston had already thought of that too, but didn't want to speak on it until she got more of the story.

"She started hallucinating when I was really young, but I didn't know at the time that that was the name of it, you know, because I was so young. I just knew she would see things all around us and there would be nothing there. Some days she wouldn't even know who I was. I don't understand how no one caught on to it before it got that bad.

"Well back then Lincoln mental illness was sort of a taboo in the black community. We didn't really seek outside help for those kinds of things."

"But if people knew she was crazy why would they leave me with her? Why wouldn't they try to help me?" he was almost pleading for answers.

"Maybe she never asked for help. I can't really answer that question." Dr. Langston felt so sorry for him because as long as she had known him, he had been searching for answers that he would most likely never get.

"All those years no one ever came to help me. I cried every day and I screamed for hours on end most days. How did no one hear any of my cries?"

He looked Dr. Langston in the eyes searching for some sort of answer. "And all the praying she did you would have thought she would have been a good godly woman, but she wasn't. I can recite the whole Bible to you, Doc, backwards and forwards and in my sleep. A lot of good that did me. The Bible is what fucked up my life. Everything I've done for God and he never came through for me, not one damn time in my life I can look back and say, yeah, God did that for me."

"How is that Lincoln?"

"My mother never saw me as anything but a sinner. I was born out of sin and she said it never left me, that sinning was embedded in my soul so she tried to kill me so I wouldn't sin anymore."

"Lincoln I am sorry that you went through all that as a child but we may never know why she did what she did, because she never asked for help. Do you know where your grandparents are?"

"Yeah I've always known where they were but I never reached out to them. Why should I? They never cared all this time, why should they care now?" He hadn't thought about his grandparents in years. When he was a child, he used to pray they would come and rescue him but they never came. He had never seen them in person, but he always heard his mother on the phone arguing with her father about cutting her out of his life and not letting her talk to her mother.

"Maybe they didn't know what was going on. I think you should reach out to them."

"Nah, when she died they didn't even come for me. That let me know then they didn't give a fuck about me."

"But a lot of years…"

"Look bitch he said he didn't want to go see them so leave him alone!"

"Hello Zachariah," Dr. Langston said catching on to the change in his voice and demeanor.

"Don't play with me, Doc. You stirring up a bunch of unnecessary shit. We are doing just fine so just leave him alone or I'll put you on the list of sinners that need to be taken care of. We work for the Lord. Are you a child of God?"

"Yes, I am, I pray and attend church every Sunday."

"The fuck is that supposed to mean 'cause you attend church?" Zachariah scoffed. "Do you know how many church hoes suck dick in the back of the pews of church?"

"But why are you so mad though?" Dr. Langston's professionalism went out the window. "You say you work for the Lord." She made the quote unquote sign with her fingers. "But you blaspheme the church. How does that work?"

"I'm not mad, Doc, I just don't sugarcoat shit. Lincoln's mother has to be the most evil woman to squat and pop a child out of a twat. She knew the Bible backwards and forwards and maybe even knew it in Hebrew. Look how much good that did for poor old Lincoln. She did everything to him but kill him, and she tried that, might I add. And he still turned out to be what she so desperately tried to kill."

"And what's that Zachariah?"

"A killer."

"Are you the killer or is Lincoln the killer?"

"Does that even matter?" He looked at her like she had six heads. "I am him, he is me, and we are one." He stood up, walked over to her, and squatted down in front of her, low enough so that they were at eye level.

"When Lincoln brings me the sinners, I punish them in unimaginable ways. Ways that would make the devil himself cringe." He regarded her to see if he saw fear in her eyes, none was showing yet, but he would change that soon enough. "Have you ever seen a human being skinned alive" She shook her head no. Dr. Langston didn't know whether to be scared or fascinated. "Well I have, have you ever seen the skin raked off of a woman's bones?" Again, she shook her head no. "The cries of sinning whoremongers sends my soul into orbits unchartered."

Dr. Langston wanted to speak but couldn't find any words. Her mind had gone blank. Zachariah had scared any comprehension right out of her.

"The sight of blood makes my dick hard and the sound of screams makes me nut even harder." He stood back up but made sure that their faces were only inches apart when he spoke. "So, Doc, don't let Lincoln confuse you on what's real. You may see a sweet tortured man. But I know the truth and you will too if you keep pressing your luck with me. I will have no problem chopping you up into little pieces while you are alive. I'm not attached to you." He laughed a little. "Poor Lincoln would never know what happened." He stood straight up, went back to where he was sitting, and winked at her. "You weren't expecting that big revelation were you sinner? If I were you, I would take heed to what the evil bastard just told you. Because I don't like you either and we both know Lincoln isn't strong enough to refuse me of my desires," Dorothy spoke terrifying Dr. Langston even more.

Dr. Langston sat unable to move. She was afraid to move or even speak. She felt like she had a load of shit waiting at the tip of her anus. At first, she was fascinated by Lincoln's situation, but Zachariah had totally creeped her out. She didn't know if she wanted to go on with Lincoln or not.

"Doc, you ok?" Lincoln asked. She looked like she had seen the devil himself.

"Lincoln?" she asked finally finding her voice and the courage to actually speak.

"Yeah, what's wrong with you?"

"So you don't remember talking to me just now?" she questioned because she wasn't sure of anything anymore.

"What are you talking about Doc?" Lincoln looked confused at first but Dr. Langston could see a light of recognition go off in his head. "She talked to you didn't she?"

"Yes and she had some pretty interesting things to say." She didn't want to mention what Zachariah had just said to her. She didn't want him to know that she knew his deepest darkest secret.

"Did you see her? I see her everywhere."

"What do you mean..." Dr. Langston stopped in the middle of her question. She realized he had no clue that he was talking as his mother. He just thought she was around him all the time.

"Why you looking at me like that Doc?" She had never looked at him like that before. She was looking at him like the other doctors used to when he was younger, like he was crazy.

"I'm just gathering my notes, that's all, Lincoln. But to answer your question no I didn't see her I just heard her." Still, Dr. Langston waited to get as much information as possible before she came up with her conclusion.

"Don't lie to me, Doc," Lincoln warned.

"I'm not lying to you Lincoln." She didn't sound convincing.

"Then tell me why you were looking at me like that!" Dr. Langston could see things were about to take a turn for the worse. She watched his facial expressions change a hundred shades of anger.

"I told you..." She couldn't finish her sentence because before she could blink, Lincoln was on his feet with his hands around her throat.

"Why you lying?" He tightened his grip on her neck. He didn't know why he had snapped but he couldn't control his anger.

"Lincoln, stop it, I can't breathe." First it was Zachariah threatening her, then Dorothy, and now Lincoln was about to choke the life right out of her.

"The worst sinner there is, is the liar," he gritted and spittle flew into her face. He was so close to her that their noses were touching. His eyes had glossed over and he had a far off look in his eyes.

"I'm not lying!" She gasped for air as she scratched at his hands.

"He that believeth on the Son hath everlasting life, and he that believeth not the Son shall not see life, but the wrath of God abideth on him."

"Lincoln..." Dr. Langston managed to get out before everything went black.

When Lincoln felt her body go flaccid, it was like something clicked in his head. He let her neck go and she fell into his arms. He wanted to cry for what he had done to Dr. Langston. She wasn't dead and he was happy for that, but would she still help him or be scared of him now. He laid her down on the couch, covered her up, and left quietly. His heart was heavy with grief because nothing would ever change in his life. He was stuck with his mother, Zachariah, and the duties he had sworn to do so long ago.

21
EVIL WITHIN

"How is everything going with you and Gabrielle?" Mike asked Lincoln as they rode down the streets patrolling the neighborhood looking for any mischief.

"It's cool, just taking some getting used to it you know." He shrugged his shoulders. "It's always just been me and now I have to think of someone else's feelings." Hurting Gabrielle was the last thing that Lincoln wanted to do. His anger was taking control of him and he couldn't blame Zachariah. After what happened with Gabrielle and Dr. Langston, he didn't trust himself around them anymore.

"It's not going to be easy but don't give up on it before it evens starts." Mike had never seen Lincoln so happy. He just hoped that Lincoln believed he deserved to be happy.

"I guess," Lincoln half-answered as someone had

caught his attention standing on the street. It was the prostitute who had called him out. He wanted to jump out and take care of her right then and there. Even though he vowed he was finished killing for the Lord, he doubted if Zachariah would go for that. He wasn't looking forward to the confrontation with his mother about his decision either.

"You listening to me man?" Mike nudged Lincoln with his elbow. He let his eyes follow Lincoln's line of vision and his eyes rested on the pimp and the prostitute that he too had been searching for.

"Huh? Yeah I'm listening," Lincoln lied. He hadn't heard a thing Mike had said he was too busy thinking about his life. He hadn't heard from his mother in a week or two and was wondering if she was gone for good. It had been years since he went that long without speaking to her. He could honestly say he didn't miss her one bit.

"I said we have to get to together maybe she can get Michelle out of the house sometimes." Mike laughed.

"Yeah maybe."

"What is going on with you man?" Mike noticed something had changed in his friend lately.

"Nothing, thinking, I got a lot on my mind." Lincoln thought about Dr. Langston. He wanted to call her but wondered if she would accept his phone call. Had she called the police on him? Did she hate him? Was she afraid of him now? It hurt him to his core to think that the one person who had always been there for him was now afraid of him.

"You want to talk about it?"

"Huh?" Lincoln looked over at Mike as if he had just realized he was still there.

"No I'm good. It's the same old shit just a different day." He turned his attention back to the street and continued watching the comings and goings of the people walking the streets of St. Louis.

"You know she has to go."

"Huh, what did you just say?" Lincoln looked over at Mike.

"I ain't said nothing." Mike looked at him quizzically

"Oh my bad, thought you said something." Lincoln went back to people watching.

"She is going to cause a lot of problems. She has to go. I want that sinner taken care of Lincoln!"

"What sinner Mother?" Lincoln finally caught on to her voice.

"The sinner you are shacking up with! She is married and an adulterer!" Dorothy fumed.

"You can to go straight to hell if you think I'm going to hurt her."

Mike watched as Lincoln had a conversation with himself. He wanted to interrupt the conversation but thought better of it. One second, he was talking in his voice, and then the next his voice would be feminine.

"How dare you speak to me like that?"

"Look, Mother, she is off limits. I've done everything you've asked of me! Now go away and let me live my life."

"Little ungrateful bastard. I knew I should have aborted you when my parents told me to."

"But you didn't so fuck off."

"Aye man you good, who the hell you talking to?" Mike was starting to get scared he pulled over on the side of the road just in case Lincoln got on some psycho type of shit. He had watched movies and had even taken a few psychology courses, but he'd never seen anything in person like he had just witnessed.

"My mother," Lincoln stated flatly.

"Your mother? Ain't nobody here but us?" Mike could remember at some point Lincoln telling him that his mother visited him often. He thought maybe Lincoln meant in dreams, but he could clearly see he was wrong.

"She's always here." Lincoln looked over at Mike. "Just be glad you haven't witnessed the madness that's in my head.

*****

Lincoln sat outside of the hotel that Gabrielle was still staying at contemplating on whether to go in or not. He had fallen in love with her and never wanted to cause her any pain. However, it seemed that his mother had set her sights on Gabrielle. He thought back to when his mother made him kill Monique and wanted to cry because he knew he wasn't strong enough to fight the urges she brought when she came around. It seemed as if his mother was determined for him to suffer his whole life.

"She's a fornicator, she must go!" Dorothy stated as if Gabrielle's life meant nothing.

"Well I fornicate with her often; does that mean I must go too Mother?"

"You will answer for your sins in due time."

"Well Gabrielle and I will cross that bridge when the time comes."

"I tried to save you from yourself."

"I'm not having this conversation with you right now. I told you she was off limits!" Lincoln's frustration showed in the tone he used.

"The Lord's will shall be done." Dorothy knew Lincoln wasn't strong enough to resist her.

"Just let me be happy for once in my life!" he yelled as he got out of his car and slammed the door. He made a mental note to tell Gabrielle to look for an apartment. He was tired of her living in a hotel. Plus, she had started to complain about her living situation also. She kept hinting around about moving into his home, but he couldn't do that, at least not any time soon.

When Lincoln walked into the hotel room, he

could see Gabrielle's naked silhouette under the sheets. The sight of her warmed his heart and his manhood instantly started to grow in his pants. He went to the bathroom and turned on the shower.

Lincoln stared into the mirror while the shower got hot. Steam filled the bathroom and placed a cloud over the mirror. He was happy the mirror was covered in steam because the reflection that was staring back at him was disturbing. He still looked the same but he felt like he was living two lives at the moment and in reality, he was. His secrets were starting to weigh heavy on his mental stability. He stepped into the shower and let the hot water run down his body.

Lincoln felt a slight draft then felt Gabrielle wrap her arms around his torso as she placed soft kisses all over his back making sure she kissed his scars. She loved every part of him and she could tell something was bothering him. She just wished he would open up to her, let her in so she could be there for him.

"Is everything ok baby?" Gabrielle asked as she rested her head on his back. He fit seamlessly in her arms. In her mind, they were the puzzle pieces that completed both their puzzles in life and love.

"Yeah everything is perfect now." He gave her hand a slight squeeze. And everything was perfect at that moment; she made everything right. He relaxed as her hands traveled up and down his chest and then rested on his hard dick. She used both hands to stroke him and she felt him shiver at the touch of her hands. He was hard as steel in her hands and she could feel the veins in his dick pulsating as she stroked him. She turned him around so that they were facing each other.

Lincoln's eyes held a sadness in them that she wanted so desperately to erase. Lincoln stared into her eyes then pulled her face into his. He kissed her so passionately it took her breath away. He had never kissed her with such passion and vigor. It almost felt like a good-bye forever kiss, but she loved how aggressive he was being. He was normally very gentle with her, but she guessed he had some stress to relieve and that's what she was there for. She would be his stress reliever if that's what he wanted.

Lincoln let her face go, went down to his knees, and he lifted her left leg up over his shoulder. The water ran all over his face as he sucked her clit into his mouth. She let out a soft moan as she grabbed the back of his head. She let her head fall back as he licked and sucked on her pussy sending shivers up and down her spine. He flicked his tongue back and forth over her clit sending intense chills up her spine. Lincoln stood up and turned her around so she was facing the shower wall. He pushed her back forward making her bend over. Bracing herself, she put her hands on the wall. He slid into her tight walls and her body tensed up. No matter how many times they had had sex his girth always took her breath away. She exhaled slowly as he filled her insides with his love pole. Lincoln dug his nails into her ass cheeks with every stroke and the deeper he went. He reached around to the front of her and began to pull and pinch her clit as he deep stroked her. She screamed as her legs began to shake from the soul shuddering orgasm but he didn't let up. He kept right on driving deep into her love box bringing on an orgasm so forceful her body went limp and he had to catch her.

Lincoln held her up as he felt that familiar feeling of the blood rushing to the tip of his dick. He wrapped his arms around her waist and drove his pole into her as he bit down on her shoulder to keep from screaming out like a woman. Her pussy felt like wet silk wrapped around his manhood. He tried to push more of his dick into her love tunnel but he was met with resistance as her walls constricted around him and he hit bottom.

Gabrielle felt his pace speed up so she knew he was on the verge of an orgasm and she moved so he would fall out of her. She got down on her knees and stared at his massive piece. She had to taste him; she was never given a chance to indulge in his chocolate goodness, but she was going to take this opportunity to taste him. The scars that adorned his phallus did nothing to deter her desire to taste to him. She took ahold of him and stuffed as much of his dick into her mouth that she could handle without choking herself. Gabrielle's hot mouth and soft hands wrapped around his dick was driving him wild. There was only one other woman that was able to satisfy him with oral sex and that was Monique.

To Lincoln's recollection, he had only been with two women. However, there was no telling what mischief Zachariah had been up to. Gabrielle was holding her own in the oral sex department. He pulled her up, lifted her up into the air, and she wrapped her legs round his waist as they walked to the bed. He gently lay her down on the bed and crawled up her body placing soft kisses all over stomach and breasts. Chills and tingles shot through her body at the touch of his lips against her skin. Once he reached her face, he stopped kissing and looked her in the eyes. For just a moment in time, everything was right in his world. If he could live in that moment forever, he would have. Gabrielle was the one thing in life Lincoln had been missing. He prayed God would let him keep her forever. There was nothing but silence as they stared into each other's eyes. Lincoln broke the silence.

"I love you." Lincoln had never said to that any woman but Ms. Jill. Gabrielle had stolen his heart from the moment he saw her. He wanted to be her everything, and it scared him to death to feel that way about her, because he had no clue how she would react if she ever found out who he really was underneath the facade he had been hiding behind.

"I love you too." Gabrielle let the tears run down the side of her face. His words hit her like a Mac truck. He had never expressed how he felt about her. She knew he felt some type of way about her because he took great care of her. She wanted for nothing and he made her feel like a real woman. It felt good to hear him say it out loud though. "My heart is yours for the taking. Just be gentle with it and don't break it." Gabrielle's heart had been broken many times over and she couldn't afford to have it broken again. Another blow to her heart would definitely end her.

"I would never do anything to hurt you or your heart." He placed his lips against hers and made passionate love to her for the rest of the night. He put all his worries out of his mind. He would enjoy the moment even as he knew deep down inside it wouldn't last long.

22
BLASPHEMY

Zachariah sat watching the comings and goings of the people of the night. Since Lincoln had taken a vow never to kill again, Zachariah had to take matters into his own hands. He knew Lincoln was only thinking with his heart and not his head. Because had he been using his brain he would have been trying to get rid of the loud mouth lady who could possibly finger him for the murders.

Zachariah didn't care how much in love Lincoln was. He would let him have his little joy, but that wouldn't do them any good if they were behind bars. The prostitute he had been looking for had just walked out of the corner store.

He had to laugh to himself because she looked a total mess, but he could tell from the way she walked you couldn't tell her she wasn't the best thing since sliced bread. She wore her signature orange lipstick with a lace cat suit and orange underwear underneath. No longer was there the blue wig, no she replaced that with a white blond short bob cut wig. He figured she was coordinating but what did he know?

Zachariah watched as a car pulled up on the side of her and as if without thinking, she jumped into the car with the person. He didn't care if she jumped in the car with Jesus himself, she had to be taken care of that night. Lately, Lincoln had been on some love is everything and nothing else matters anymore type of shit.

The John parked his car in the alley. Zachariah turned his headlights out as he pulled into the alley behind them. He could see the prostitute's head go down so he knew what she was doing.

He got out of the car and walked up on the driver's side of the car. The window was down.

"Mmmmm suck that dick you bitch," Zachariah heard the John say. Her head moved up and down at a vigorous speed. So much so, he almost hated to interrupt the session, but he had to get things moving along.

"You like that daddy?" she questioned with her jaws filled with dick and balls.

"Ye…" his answer was cut short when Zachariah reached in, grabbed his head, and sliced his throat in one swift motion. The John got off easy in Zachariah's eyes. He had seen the wedding ring on his finger. Being out there at night with a prostitute made him an adulterer and he should have been punished accordingly.

The prostitute felt something wet hit her face. She knew it couldn't have been semen because the man's dick was in her mouth.

"You drooling on me and shit!" She stopped her yelling when she saw his throat had been slashed from ear to ear. She looked around and at her hands, saw all the blood everywhere, and immediately went to reach for the door. Zachariah stuck his stun gun into the window and shot it at her stopping her in her tracks.

*****

Mike had been following who he thought was Lincoln, and much to his dismay, he watched as Lincoln had sliced the throat of the man in the driver's seat. For a while, Mike had thought that Lincoln had been up to something but he never did he think this was it. Lincoln's demeanor was always a little dark but he also had a jovial spirit behind it all.

Mike watched in horror as Lincoln dragged the prostitute out of the car and threw her into the back of his car. He went to reach for his walkie-talkie but stopped. He wanted to see where this would lead. In addition, he didn't know what state of mind Lincoln was in. He didn't want to make a mistake and get the woman killed.

*****

When Greg made Gabrielle stop all communication with her family, she was devastated. The look of pain on her mother's face haunted her every day.

"Gabrielle bring your ass on!" Greg yelled as he and Gabrielle's mother stood toe to toe in a deathly standoff. Neither one of them had plans on backing down.

"You're a loser and a coward. Preying on young and naïve girls." She laughed in his face.

"Well if you hadn't been such a fucked up mother she wouldn't be so naïve now would she?" he returned the laughter.

"Please stop it, don't do this!" Gabrielle pleaded she didn't know what to do. She was stuck between the two people that meant the most to her, her husband and her mother. Here her mother stood defending her honor when she had never had the courage to defend her own honor. How she wished she had inherited her mother's strength.

"I'll show you a fucked up mother if you put your hands on her while she is in front of me. Please try me." The threat was clear in her eyes as she held on to a steel bat in her hands.

"Like I said, come the fuck on Gabby." Gabrielle went to walk away with Greg but her mother grabbed her by the arm.

"You don't have to go with him baby. Stay with your family sweetheart." She rubbed the sides of Gabrielle's face tenderly. She had tears running down her face as she spoke. It broke her heart to watch her daughter go through so much mental and physical abuse.

"Ma he's my husband," Gabrielle pleaded.

"He's a coward and punk that puts his hands on you. Baby that is no way live. You are such a beautiful woman. You deserve better."

"I'm sorry, Ma, I have to go. I'll call you later ok?"

"No she won't." Greg laughed as he pulled her out of the front door.

That had been the last time Gabrielle had seen or talked to her mother or anyone in her family. Greg would beat her within an inch of her life every time she would mention her family.

She picked up the hotel room phone and made a call she had been terribly afraid of making. The phone rang four times before she heard a deep baritone voice speak.

"Hello?"

Hello Jay Jay?" Gabrielle asked making sure it was her big brother on the other end of the phone.

"Yeah who is this?"

"Gabby."

"Gabby who?"

"How many Gabby's you know?" she joked trying to make light of the tense situation. At least it was tense for her. She was nervous and afraid of rejection.

"Oh shit, hey everybody Gabby is on the phone!" he yelled excitedly to everyone in the house with him.

"Tell everyone I said hi!" She was relieved they weren't mad at her. She had held off on calling them, too afraid they would hate her for leaving. "Where is Ma?" She noticed her mother hadn't said anything in the background or snatched the phone from him.

"Um…"

"Um what Jay?" She could tell there was something he was hesitant to say. Before he spoke the words, there was a warm feeling that took over her body.

"Sis she died from a massive heart attack 2 years ago," he said somberly.

"What?" she shrieked.

"Yeah we reached out and called you to let you know, but Greg said no one in his household cared and for us never to call his home again. Then he blocked all our calls and moved you away."

"She died and he didn't tell me?" she cried into the phone.

"Yeah that son a bitch is foul," her brother stated heatedly.

"He was foul."

"What you do mean was?"

"He's dead and good riddance."

"What? When?"

"We will get into all that when I visit you all this weekend."

"Ok sis I can't wait to see you. We've missed you around here."

"Ok I love you."

"Love you too."

After Gabrielle got off the phone with her brother, she sat dumbfounded. She couldn't believe that Greg would be that cruel to keep such important information from her. What kind of person wouldn't tell someone their mother had passed away?

"I knew he was a sick evil bastard, but never that evil," she said out loud to herself as she shook her head.

Gabrielle sat staring at the computer screen. Lincoln's home address stared back her in a taunting way. She knew that going through such lengths to find out where he lived, was borderline stalkerish.

Gabrielle hadn't seen nor heard from Lincoln in a week and instead of being worried, she was pissed. She'd called his phone multiple times with no answer or response, so in true woman private investigator mode; she went to the internet to find him. She still had his credit card information. She got into the site and found out the address that was associated with the card. She hoped it was still current.

If she found him with another woman she was going to go ape shit on him. She had been through too much in her life and she was not letting him go without a fight. She jotted down the address, grabbed her purse and keys, and was on her way to find out what was going on with Lincoln.

*****

When orange lips woke up, she was naked and handcuffed to a chair with a high back and her neck was strapped to the back of the chair. She looked around but couldn't move too much. The strap gave her just enough room to breathe. She yanked at the handcuffs to no avail. Frantically, she looked around to see if anyone was there with her.

"Hello?" She was met with silence. "Hello!" she yelled. "Is anyone there? What is this place? Where am I?"

"You are at the gates of hell sinner," Zachariah said as he stepped out of a dark corner of the shed. He had been sitting watching her for about ten minutes patiently waiting for her to wake up or his surprise guest to show up. Zachariah knew tonight was going to change Lincoln's life forever.

Mike had followed Zachariah home and he couldn't let Mike leave knowing what he now knew. He knew how close Lincoln and Mike were and he honestly would have never hurt Mike had he just minded his own business. Knowing Mike was on his way in at any moment he didn't have time to do his torture thing. However, he still had something special planned for the loud-mouthed lady. Because if it weren't for her, he wouldn't be in the position he was in at the moment.

"What is your name sinner?"

"Huh, excuse me?"

"What is your name?"

"My name is Keisha and you're that pig I was telling Daddy Kool Aid about!"

"Well kinda sorta. I mean he's me and not me at the same time. You understand?"

"Unhandcuff me muthafucka!

"In due time bitch," Zachariah said as he walked up to her with thick work gloves and a razor sharp wire in his hands. As he was wrapping it around her neck, he heard something outside the door.

"Looks like the party is just about to get started." He smiled and winked at her. He grabbed a roll of duct tape, broke a piece off, and slapped it across her face with force. So hard, she felt a tooth fly to the back of her throat. Zachariah crept to the back of the door and waited for Mike to enter.

Mike crept into the shed slowly, careful not to make any noise. He thought he had heard voices but when he looked in, all he could see was the prostitute sitting in the middle of the shed gagged, naked, and chained to a chair.

"Oh my God, what the hell is going on here?" he questioned as he ran to free her from her restraints. He was too busy trying to free her that he didn't notice her trying to get his attention.

"Mmmmm," she mumbled as she threw her head frantically from side to side. "Mmmmmm!" She shook the chair but he wouldn't look up. She watched Zachariah as he leaned against the wall smiling at her. His smile sent chills up her spine and tears instantly started running freely down her face. There was something in his smile that let her know that things were about to get real bad.

*****

Gabrielle had pulled into Lincoln's driveway a few minutes after Mike. She watched as he walked up to a shed in the backyard. She stayed back careful not to get spotted lurking in dark. She felt kind of foolish for thinking he was with another woman. However, she'd learned you couldn't put anything past anyone. She looked around and rubbed her arms as a chill circulated through her body. She looked around cautiously. The darkness of the woods was starting to creep her out. She sat down on his porch to give Mike and Lincoln time to do whatever they were doing. She didn't want to interrupt in case they were doing something important considering the fact that she wasn't supposed to even be there.

*****

"Just calm down ma'am. I'm going to get you out of here." Mike pulled at the handcuffs. "Shit!" he cursed as he pat himself down looking for something to help get her loose.

"Mmmmm!" Keshia screamed under the tape. Please God let him take the tape off my mouth, she thought. She could clearly see her prayers weren't going to be answered that day, because Zachariah had just slipped up to the back of Mike.

"I really wish you wouldn't have done that." Mike turned to the voice that came from behind him and was met with a hammer to his temple.

*****

Dr. Langston sat halfway listening to her newest patient explain what it felt like to suffer from formication. He hallucinated that insects were crawling all over his body and under his skin.

"Dr. Langston do you think they have exterminators for this type of infestation?" he asked as he clawed at his forearms continuously.

Dr. Langston caught herself before she answered his question. Sometimes, she found herself wanting to ask, "Mothufucker are you kidding me?"

"No there are no exterminators for this condition. But I have some medicine I will prescribe to you that will help you," she answered as she unconsciously scratched the skin on her neck. She

was ready for him to make his exit. All the
scratching he was doing was starting play tricks on
her mind. She'd begin to think insects were
crawling on her and she knew there weren't any
around.

The patient continued talking about his
infestation problems but Dr. Langston's mind had
wandered off. She wondered what Lincoln had been
doing since the last time she'd seen him. Had he
and Zachariah been out killing again? Where was he
at, at that very moment? She thought about
Zachariah and Dorothy's threat and that helped her
keep her distance from Lincoln. The look in
Lincoln's eye's that night gave her nightmares for
days. She rubbed at the bruises that were finally
leaving her neck that Lincoln put there when he
choked her. No matter how much she wanted to
help Lincoln, it was he who had tried to choke the
life out of her; he couldn't blame Zachariah nor
Dorothy.

23
Thy Will

"Look what you made me do!" Zachariah yelled at Keisha. He would have never hurt Mike because he was Lincoln's only friend in the world. Now, because of loud mouth he had to get rid of him too. "You made me do this so you're going to watch this and you should pray that yours is this quick." He glanced her way to make sure she was watching. No matter how much of a killer he was, he meant what he said when he had said that he and Lincoln were one, and his only mission in life was to protect Lincoln from any pain.

"Please don't do this," Mike whispered as he watched Zachariah tower over him like a dark cloud of death.

Zachariah paused and stared at Mike as he kept a tight grip on the hammer he had been holding in his hand. Zachariah looked back and forth between Mike and Keisha and felt rush of rage flow through his body.

"Why couldn't you just," he walked over to her,

"keep your fucking mouth shut?" he gritted as he swung the hammer connecting with her mouth. Instantly, she began to choke as teeth and blood ran down the back of her throat. "No you won't die that easily bitch!" He snatched the tape off her mouth and blood spilled from between her lips. She gasped for air as she threw up blood, teeth, and whatever food she had eaten that day. Both her lips had swollen up to almost five times their regular size and they were split down the middle displaying the fatty meat that was once covered by the skin of her lips.

Tears and mucus ran from her eyes and nose as she watched Zachariah walk back over to Mike. If it was really her fault that they were in that predicament, she was truly sorry and regretted ever opening her mouth.

Zachariah looked down at Mike and regarded him as he got in his swinging stance. They locked eyes and anger was evident in Mike's eyes.

"Please know that Lincoln didn't do this to you, I did, and he would never agree to let me do this. He loves you like a brother." Zachariah felt himself getting choked up at the thought of the pain Lincoln was going to be in.

"Please, I swear, I won't say anything," Mike pleaded. He wasn't ready to leave his family. What would they tell his wife and kids? That their Godfather killed their father? How would his children understand that? His sweet Michelle, he would never get to see her smile again, hold her again, or feel the softness of her flesh under his touch. His death would devastate his family; never in a million years did he think Lincoln would be the one to take his life. He dealt with killers, psychos, and drug dealers on a daily basis. Never did he think he would die at the hands of his best friend.

"I'm sorry." Zachariah watched as hurt and defeat flashed in Mike's eyes. Mike was too disorientated to fight back or even get up. Zachariah swung the hammer again connecting with Mike's forehead, killing him instantly.

"Look at what you made me do!" Zachariah yelled again. He walked over and snatched Keisha by her hair so she was looking at Mike's mutilated face. He lay dead in front of her with his face beaten in so badly it was unrecognizable. The bone structure in Mike's face had been beaten to mush. "Open your eyes," Zachariah whispered in her face once he noticed she refused to look at his handiwork. "Open your eyes bitch." He bit down on her cheek hard, drawing blood. "Open your fucking eyes!"

"No you sick son a bitch!" Keisha cried.

Zachariah let go of her face and walked over to the shelf where all his toys were on display. Keisha watched as he picked up an icepick and slid something else in his back pocket. She watched his every move intently terrified of what was to come next. He was covered in Mike's blood and had a crazed far off look in his eyes. She noticed the V-neck shirt he wore showed off a zipper shaped scar going across his neck. To her, he seemed to be moving in slow motion as he walked back over to her and pressed his face firmly against hers. She tried to avoid looking in his eyes but she couldn't pull her eyes away. His eyes bore holes through her soul, as if he could see all of the sins she had ever committed.

"I don't like repeating myself. That means you are being disobedient."

"Please just let me go!" Keisha cried. His breath was so hot it felt like he was breathing fire as he talked to her. She kept her eyes clenched shut refusing to see what was coming next. On the few occasions that she actually opened her eyes, she was mortified at what she saw. She had stepped into a horror movie designed just for her, staring her, and ending with her.

"There is no letting you go sinner." He stood up tall, towering over her. "If you would have just shut your big mouth none of us would be here. I mean you may have eventually ended up on our list, but poor Mike would be home with his wife and kids. Lincoln would be somewhere getting some ass and all would be well in the world." He shook his head. "So you see bitch you are never leaving!" he yelled as brought his foot up and kicked her in the chest sending her and the chair flying backwards.

She had barely hit the floor before he was on top of her, ramming the icepick into the area between her shoulder and collarbone. He pulled the pear of anguish out of his back pocket and jammed it into her mouth when she screamed out.

The pear he held in his hand was a remake of the

medieval torture device that was used as punishment and inserted into the orifices of liars, blasphemers, prostitutes, and homosexuals to mutilate the walls of the vagina or anus.

"Did you know they used these on the whores back in the good ole days?" Zachariah asked more as a comment than a question. He watched her attentively as she struggled to take breaths. Tears ran down her face, as she looked death in the eyes. "Yeah they would jam this here pear shaped thing in their rotten cunts and twist this little screw here, like so." He began twisting the screw at the top of the pear and it began to expand like a blooming rosebud in her mouth. Keisha shook her head from side to side, as she felt the pressure of the metal pressing up against the roof of her mouth. The metal cut into the meat in her mouth as the pear spread further sending excruciating pain radiating through her face. She silently prayed for death to come on swift wings and take her away.

"Wherefore I say unto you, all manner of sin and blasphemy shall be forgiven unto men: but the blasphemy against the Holy Spirit." Zachariah clenched his teeth as he recited the scripture and watched her teeth shatter as the pear spread to it limits. Her body bucked and she shook her head trying her best to get him off her. With one more twist of the screw, the bones in her face shattered and penetrated her brain. "Shall not be forgiven unto men."

24
My Life

Gabrielle felt like she had given Lincoln and Mike long enough time do whatever they were doing in the shed. She turned the knob and walked in.

"Babe I'm sorry but," her sentence stopped when she saw Mike's dead corpse lying in a pool of blood. Then she looked over and could see Lincoln hunched over a woman's body. She screamed at the top of her lungs and dashed out of the shed with Zachariah hot on her heels.

"Where did Lincoln meet you nosy muthafuckas damn?" Zachariah yelled as he closed the distance between him and Gabrielle.

Gabrielle looked back just in time to see him swing the shovel he had picked up on his way out of the shed. Her instincts to duck didn't kick in fast enough and he connected with the back of her head knocking her out.

Zachariah sat Indian style covered in blood in front of Gabrielle waiting for her to wake up. She was a beautiful lady and Zachariah could clearly see why Lincoln had fallen for her. Though her beauty shined bright, it was the blood running down over her shoulder from the blow to her head that had his excitement at an all-time high.

Never in a million years, did Zachariah think she would have shown up at the house while he was doing what he did best. He knew one day his and Lincoln's worlds would collide, but not like this. Now, he found himself in his own nightmare. He knew Lincoln would break if he killed her but he also knew they couldn't go to jail or back to the psychiatric ward.

Zachariah and Lincoln's time in the hospital was the worst time period of their lives. The smell of feces and urine wafted through the halls most likely due to one of the patients having a tantrum and either throwing it on one of the workers or going on themselves. The sight of the psychotic patients pacing back and forth beating themselves in the head and mumbling incoherently to themselves was an everyday vision for Zachariah and he never wanted to relive that again.

Zachariah shook his head at the thought of what he was about to do. How had things gotten so fucked up in one night? Had he known Mike was following, he would have never gotten the prostitute and just waited for another time, but he had already gotten her by the time he noticed Mike trailing him. He looked over at Mike and felt a twinge of guilt.

What had he done? Was he helping Lincoln or making things worse?

"Why did you have to show up here?" he asked out loud to himself. "You couldn't just stay a good little house wife?" he asked as he looked back to Gabrielle.

"Lin…Lincoln what is this?" Gabrielle questioned as she started to come to. She reached her for aching head but was met with resistance. Her vision was hazy and her head spun at an alarming speed as she tried to focus on the figure sitting in front of her.

Gabrielle's vision began to clear up enough for her to take in her surroundings. Mike lay in a pool of blood with his face smashed in and a dead lady stared at her with hollow eyes. She looked over to the deceased lady and it looked like her mouth had been turned inside out. Then Gabrielle's eyes landed on Zachariah covered in blood from head to toe sitting in front of her.

Neither of them spoke a word; both were trying to feel the other out. The air in the room was thick with tension leaving a feeling that the air had been vacuumed out of the room.

"Where is Lincoln?" Gabrielle asked. She knew deep down in her soul that the man sitting in front of her was not her love. When Lincoln was in her presence, she felt nothing but love radiating from him. The figure sitting in front of her was emitting a hatred so strong he could have been the devil himself.

"Very perceptive Gabby." He smiled at her. "Can I call you Gabby?" She didn't answer; she just stared at him. She wondered how she hadn't known what was really going on with Lincoln. He had so many secrets and buried feelings, but she thought she was getting through to him. Never would she have guessed that this was one of his secrets. "See Gabby we find ourselves in quite a predicament."

"And what predicament is that?" She knew from the scene in front of her that she should have been scared shitless, but she felt in her heart that Lincoln would never do anything to hurt her. With everything laid out in front her, she only wanted to love Lincoln even more.

"Those two found out about me and Lincoln's little secret. I never wanted to hurt Mike though; I actually liked ole Mikey for Lincoln. He brought a certain comradery that Lincoln never had before, you know?"

"Who are you?"

"Oh we haven't formally met yet have we?" He smiled at her. "I'm Zachariah; I won't get into the extra details of what that means. But I honestly do wish we could have met under better circumstances." He stood up. "You know at a family BBQ, church, Christmas. But we have to play the cards dealt to us." He shrugged his shoulders. "But one good thing about knowing somebody who knows somebody is that you get to bypass the torture."

"Lincoln…"

"I am Lincoln, we are."

"Lincoln I know you can hear me!" She cut
Zachariah off not wanting to hear a word he had to
say.

"He can't save you."

"Lincoln, baby, don't let him do this to us.
You're stronger than him," Gabrielle cried.

"I would save my breath if I were you. You don't
have much longer to have the privilege of doing
such a thing as breathing."

"Lincoln, baby, please hear me!"

"He can't hear you! Now you are starting to piss
me off!"

"He's stronger than you; he won't let you hurt
me."

"But he's not stronger than me sinner!" Dorothy
said as she jammed the icepick that Zachariah had
been playing with into Gabrielle's thigh.

Gabrielle screamed. "Why!" The icepick had
gone clear through her leg and an indescribable pain
surged through her leg. She didn't know if it was
the icepick or the fact that another man that she
loved was causing her a great deal of pain again.
"Lincoln, Lincoln, please come back to me! Help
me! Help me!" Gabrielle was hysterical at the pain
and the realization that Lincoln may not able to help
her set in.

Lincoln looked around at all the carnage that had
obviously taken place. There was blood

everywhere, even all over him. He examined his hands and they were covered in blood, whose blood was the question. Loud shrieks broke his concentration. When he looked in the direction of the screams, his heart almost stopped beating. He had to be hallucinating again. That wasn't Gabrielle in front of him bleeding and tied to a chair. The look of terror in her eyes let him know that this was real.

"Gabby?" he questioned almost inaudible, praying she was just a figment of his imagination.

"Yes, Lincoln, baby it's me. Please help me," she cried.

"Oh my God! What did he do to you?" He frantically pulled at her restraints. "I'm so sorry baby."

"Just get me loose, please, before he comes back."

"I'm so sorry."

"You didn't do this but I need you to look over there." Gabrielle nodded her head to where Mike lay dead.

When Lincoln's eyes landed on Mike's dead body, his heart felt like it had collapsed. He fell to his knees and skulked over to Mike. He lifted Mike's head and placed it in his lap. He wept for his friend.

"Why did he do this?" Lincoln asked out loud, as he rocked back and forth holding on to Mike for dear life. "I did everything they asked me to do. I led the sheep to slaughterhouse, never questioned my part." He looked up at Gabrielle. "What happened?"

"He said that Mike found out about you and his secrets?" She shifted her gaze to the floor; the agony in his eyes tore at the strings to her heart. Why wasn't she angry with him? Why wasn't she trying to fight for her life? Why was she frightened? She didn't know the answer to any of the questions in her head.

Lincoln looked back down into Mike's lifeless eyes. "Why couldn't you just leave well enough alone brother? We were only helping." He sat in a trance until he felt a hand on his shoulder.

"Zachariah had no right to take that man's life Lincoln."

"Shut up, you don't know what you are talking about." Lincoln's pain went deep into his soul but he knew Zachariah would have never killed Mike if there weren't a cause for it. He needed answers what did Mike do to warrant a death sentence?

"Baby," Gabrielle touched his shoulder. She had managed to limp over to him. Lincoln snatched away from her.

"Don't touch me! Just go away before I can't stop them anymore." He had found a spot on the wall and locked his eyes there. He rocked in a daze, stunned to silence. His heart ached because he couldn't understand why Zachariah would try to take the only people in the world that mattered to him away from him.

"But…"

"But shit!" He jumped to his feet letting Mike's head fall to the floor with a loud thud. Gabrielle jumped back, scared and unsure if it was Lincoln or Zachariah in front of her. "Look around you, this is me! This is my life!" he yelled.

"No this is not you," she pleaded. "That was not you talking to me." She reached out to touch him but he pulled away again.

"The fuck is you not getting? Are you mental or something? This is me, this is my life, and this is my world!" He waved his hands around crazily. "And nothing but death is going to change that." He stopped talking to let his own words sink in. His chest heaved in an out as if he had just run a marathon. "This is my life baby…This is my life!" He pounded on his chest with each word.

Gabrielle felt the need to reach out and touch him again but thought better of it. She wanted so badly to comfort him.

"Look at Mike. What is his family supposed to do now? He has a wife and kids, he was good man." Lincoln shook his head again. "Just stay away from me before they hurt you even worse than this time." He backed up slowly, out the door. Looking at her one last time, he let his tears flow freely down his face. Just when he thought everything was starting to flow effortlessly his whole world caved in on him in one night.

Lincoln ran as fast as he could to his car. He needed to see Dr. Langston. He needed someone to save him from himself.

25
FATHER FORGIVE ME FOR I HAVE SINNED

Lincoln raced through the streets of St. Louis trying to get to Dr. Langston's office. He was in shock from the carnage he had awakened to. Mike was dead and he had come to just in time to save Gabrielle from whatever fate Zachariah had conjured up for her. Lincoln knew his life as he once knew it was over. He prayed that Mike's family would be ok. He knew they would never understand why his own best friend killed him. He shook his head to get the horrid sight out of his mind. The hurt that showed in Gabrielle's eyes pained his soul. He never wanted to be the reason for her crying tears of pain.

Lincoln pulled up to the office building and almost jumped out the car before he even put it in park. He parked halfway in the street and half on the curb, and then rushed into the building.

"Excuse me sir you can't park right there, especially like that!" a secretary yelled as she jumped out of her seat and ran from behind her desk.

"You move it then bitch!" Lincoln threw her his keys then proceeded to the stairs taking them two at a time. He could hear her yelling for him to come back but he ignored her pleas. Dr. Langston's office was on the tenth floor. He ascended the steps with the agility of a hurdle jumper.

"Is the doctor in?" Lincoln asked as he walked through the reception area door but never paused his stride.

"Yes but you can't just go in there…" The secretary's sentence was cut short when Lincoln turned around with a pistol pointed at her head.

"Why the fuck do y'all keep trying to stop me from seeing her? Did she tell you not to let me in?" he roared as stared into her eyes searching for answers. He pushed the gun into the middle of her forehead. The lady pissed her pants and immediately started to cry.

"No sir sh…sh…she's in there with another patient," she stuttered.

"You sure that's it?" He searched her eyes for any lies. He watched the scared woman for a few more seconds then put the gun down by his side. He felt like everyone was out to get him and keep him from ever being happy. She nodded her head at him. "Well fuck him, he gots to go!" He turned and marched towards the door.

Lincoln burst through the door looking around like a crazed maniac. As soon as he saw her, a calm washed over his body. Dr. Langston had always had that calmative effect on him.

"Doc why haven't you been answering my calls?" he asked as he lifted the frightened teen out of his seat, pushed him towards the door, and waved his hand signaling for him to leave. The young man had no problems with leaving. He looked Lincoln up and down and figured Lincoln had been on a killing spree or had just started one by all the blood that coated his body. As the teen walked out the door, Lincoln locked it behind him, and then turned his attention back to Dr. Langston.

"I've been busy Lincoln." Dr. Langston hadn't seen Lincoln since the incident when he choked her until she passed out. She knew it was Lincoln who had put had put his hands on her because Zachariah would have made himself known. She had never been scared of Lincoln until that day. She had gotten attached to Lincoln and his story, but a good story wasn't worth her life. What if he couldn't control what he did the next time?

"Cops sure do come quickly around these parts." He laughed as he watched his comrades surround the building getting ready to kill him on demand. He couldn't be mad because that was his job only a day earlier. However, all that turned to shit when Zachariah decided to kill everyone he loved. Now he had no job, no family, no Gabrielle. He knew deep down he would never be able to live a happily ever after with Gabrielle.

"Lincoln why have you come here with a gun and covered in blood for that matter?" Dr. Langston tried her best to stay calm. She'd been a psychiatrist for years and thought she had seen it all, but it was

Lincoln who was taking her through every emotion her body could go through. She felt great sorrow for him but at that moment, fear had a death grip on her heart. She stood there in her office dressed in her Sunday best sweating like a runaway slave. Lincoln looked like a wild maniac covered in blood holding a gun.

"I came to apologize for what happened and to see why you haven't been answering my phone calls Doc." He scratched the side of his head with the barrel of the gun. "Why would you abandon me when I needed you most?"

"I told you I've been busy Lincoln. I have a new client list that I have to get through," she lied as she fidgeted with imaginary dust on her suit.

"That's bullshit and you know it! You've never been too busy to help me, never, not once have you ever not returned nor answered my phone calls."

"Lincoln I know you remember what you did to me." She watched him as his head dropped and his chin hit his chest.

"My apologies Doc." He looked up at her with tear-filled eyes. Confusion coated his face. "Doc things have gotten way out of hand and I don't know what to do anymore." He stood with his shoulders hunched as he looked out the window again. His fellow comrades were gearing up for war out there. He wondered if they knew it was him, if they would still be ready to shoot first then ask questions later.

"Lincoln why don't you just surrender? They are

going to kill you if they have to come in here." Dr.
Langston was frantic. No matter what he had done
to her, she would never wish death on him. She
knew he had been a tortured soul for years.

"I'm sorry Doc, I'm so sorry for what I've done,
for what we've done. I came to confess my sins to
you."

"I'm not God and I am not a pastor," she
reasoned. "I can't absolve you of your sins." She
regarded him trying to see through to his soul, but
all she saw was a hollow darkness in his eyes.

"I know who you are Doc, you're my savior. You
will be the keeper of all my secrets. You will be the
one to tell my side of the story. Let the world know
that I, Lincoln, was not a total monster. Tell them
that I did have a heart and that I loved, laughed, and
lived life to the best of my ability."

"Lincoln you will be here to tell your own
story."

"Nah, Doc, I can't live like this no more. I need
you to tell my momma that I'm sorry. I wasn't the
angel she thought I was. I never meant to hurt her."
He knew that his death would kill Jill. However, the
thought of having to sit through a trail and watch
her have to listen to all the gory details of what he
and Zachariah had been doing would have been
worse than a death sentence.

Thoughts of Gabrielle ran through Lincoln's
mind and brought him down to his knees. The
thought of never feeling her touching him again or
never smelling her scent again hurt his soul. She

was the only person in his crazy messed up world that made him totally happy. Lincoln cried. "The only woman I loved with all my heart. He took her away from me." He grabbed his face and wept for his lost love. Even if he lived through the night, he would be going to jail or even worse, a psychiatric hospital and neither place would put her in his arms.

"Who Zachariah?" Dr. Langston asked.

"Don't bring his name up right now," Lincoln stood to his feet.

"Why not? He is a part of you and the reason we are even here in the situation in the first place."

Lincoln's eyes narrowed into tiny slits. "He was not there the day I made my vow to God. He never made me do anything I didn't want to do. He protected me from everyone. I am not mad at him for what he did; I just have to deal with it and live with it."

"What about Dorothy? Do you not blame her either?"

"No that crazy bitch is the root of all this evil. Most days I wonder if she even gave birth to me."

"Lincoln…"

"Doc just leave it alone. What's done is done. Can't rewind the hands of time."

"I'm sorry, Lincoln, I thought I could help you if I had a better understanding of what was going on, but it seems I was of no use. I'm sorry I failed you."

"Could you have stopped him? Could we have

worked together to get rid of him?" He shook his head. "I don't know that I would have wanted you to help get of Zachariah."

"I understand. He has been a strong fixture in your life for years. So of course, it would have been hard to get rid of him. But you and I both know it needed to be done."

"Yeah you're right, but a little too late. Now everyone I love is gone. So all this conversation is for nothing, because it's not going to bring Mike back to life and it's not going take away the pain that I've caused Gabrielle."

"Don't give up, Lincoln; you can still do some good in the world."

"I thought I was doing good in the world. I was getting rid of all the sinners. I was a soldier in the Lord's war on sinners. What's better than that?" Dr. Langston looked away unable to meet his questioning gaze. "You know when I came around today the first thing I saw was the love of my life handcuffed to a chair bleeding from wounds I caused her. And the second thing I saw was my best friend dead from bodily harm I had caused." He pounded on the side of his head to get the images out of his mind.

Dr. Langston walked over to the window. From the looks of things, she knew they didn't have much time. The building was totally surrounded. She watched as snipers got into position to take aim at the window they were standing in front of.

They were going to take him down with full

force, but if she could get him out alive, she would do everything in her power to do so. Lincoln didn't deserve the cards he had been dealt. His whole life had been one nightmare after another and she refused to watch him get shot down like a rabid dog over the things that other people had inflicted on him. Life dealt him a no win hand and in the end, it made him the monster that he had become.

"Doc we've been killing for years. I've been killing people for years, and I don't mean shooting folks in the head, none of that simple bullshit. I mean H.H Holmes, Ed Gean, the dude from the movie "Saw" type of killing. I'm a killer," he confessed.

"You mean Zachariah is a killer right?"

"No, I mean I am a killer. I can't blame everything on him. When I was younger my mother came to me and told me that the Lord had chosen me to be the wrath of the Lord and that it was my duty to get rid of all the sinners." He shook his head "And I did as I was told until she made me kill the first woman I ever loved. Something happened to me that day; I refused to kill anymore, and that's when Zachariah took over where I left off. I brought them to the slaughterhouse with no questions asked. Hell, I even built the torture devices he used." Lincoln could see the look of horror on Dr. Langston's face. "Are you afraid of me now Doc?"

"Is that really a fair request, Lincoln, look what you just told me?" She took a few steps away from him.

"Here are my house keys. I want you to be the one to see everything. I want you to feel what it was like to be in the shed, the smell of blood and death. And please tell my story the way it should be told."

Dr. Langston watched as a red dot landed on Lincoln's chest. Lincoln followed her eyes to the dot.

"Don't you worry about them, focus on me." She moved quickly to step in front of the beam the sniper had trained on him.

"Doc before I die can you tell me what is wrong with me?"

"Lincoln I looked over all my notes and did a little research. I believe your mother was schizophrenic and may have passed it on to you. However, you also have Dissociative Identity Disorder, which is another term for split personality. But it can be helped with the right treatments." Dr. Langston spoke quickly trying to tell him as much as possible. Lincoln had been keeping her hostage for over an hour and she knew they didn't have much time because it looked like the police were getting an itchy trigger finger.

"I'll tell you when I came along Doc."

"Zachariah?" Dr. Langston noticed the change in Lincoln's demeanor and figured he was no longer there.

"Yes it is I, Zachariah, the memory of the Lord, the will of thy Lord, and the wrath of thy Lord."

"Why do you…" Her sentence was cut short

when she heard banging on the door. Next, she saw ropes hanging outside her office windows. They were coming in and there was nothing she could do to stop it.

"They are coming for us. They don't understand what we've done for them."

"Look, Zachariah, Lincoln, whichever one you are right now, just put the gun down and get down on the floor so they won't kill you, please!" Dr. Langston had never been in a situation like that before. She knew what she was trained to do but her heart wouldn't let her.

"Let them come in, we have nothing left to live for."

"What about Jill?"

"Lincoln would never do this to her." The windows to the office shattered and glass flew everywhere. The office door came crashing in followed by what seemed like a hundred police officers with their guns aimed at Lincoln. Lincoln took aim at them with no intention of ever pulling the trigger; he just wanted everything to be over.

"Wait! Dr. Langston screamed as she ran towards Lincoln to jump in front of him again, but she was too late as one of the officers tackled her to the ground. A barrage of bullets tore through Lincoln's flesh. He dropped to his knees never breaking eye contact with Dr. Langston. She screamed at the top of lungs. Seeing Lincoln die in front of her was the most horrible thing, she had ever witnessed. He took his last breath staring into her eyes.

*****

"So, Dr. Langston, Zachariah never got a chance to tell you where he had come from did he?"

"No he didn't but Lincoln had gone through so much in life he could have come from any one of the traumatic events in Lincoln's life. He could have come from the beatings, the killing of his mother, or the death of his first girlfriend Monica," Dr. Langston explained to her class.

Since Lincoln's death, she had quit the psychiatry profession and decided to become a teacher to help people learn more about the inner workings of a serial killer. Her whole course was based on Lincoln and his life story. She had written the book about his life and based the whole syllabus around the book. She'd gone through Lincoln's home and shed as he had asked her to. The death of Lincoln really hit her hard. Dr. Langston had ended up taking a hiatus after that night and never returned to her profession. After the crime scene investigators were finished going through Lincoln's home, they had found the DNA of 39 people and the bones of an estimated 20 victims down in the lake behind his home. Lincoln Zachariah Donaldson had become one of the world's most prolific serial killers ever known.